ROASTING
MARSHMALLOWS

ROASTING
MARSHMALLOWS

A Soldier's Memoir of Iraq.

DAN ALANIZ

authorHOUSE®

AuthorHouse™
1663 Liberty Drive
Bloomington, IN 47403
www.authorhouse.com
Phone: 1-800-839-8640

First published by AuthorHouse   12/27/2011

ISBN: 978-1-4678-7301-7 (sc)
ISBN: 978-1-4678-7302-4 (ebk)

Library of Congress Control Number: 2011960736

Printed in the United States of America

ACKNOWLEDGEMENTS

My greatest accomplishments have been the ones where I have been able to thank those who helped me put one foot in front of the other or stop me from inserting foot into mouth. With much regret and aching pain I will never be able to thank most of those who gave me the privilege to write these words. Those brave men who gave their lives for me and their Country, America and Iraq. SSG Christopher Moudry, SPC Timothy Burke, David my Friend and Interpreter, CPT Shawn English, Chief Warrant Ali, all of our Interpreters in whom I must change their names and darken the faces of all Iraqis to protect their friends, families, and relatives from being kidnapped and tortured as was David.

To my Military Transition Team, 2/9 Iraqi Army BDE, Scorpion members: Stanley, Ross, Marlon, Anthony, Mark, and Ernie who I wanted to thank wholeheartedly when we left FT Hood but everyone left in a hurry.

I am in debt to Lion-9th Iraqi Army DIV MiTT, 2/9 IA BNs VooDoo, Force, Highlander, and Pain. The men and women of 4th ID, 7-10 CAV (Lancers), 1-1 CAV, 1-7 CAV (Garryowen), and Phoenix Academy for supporting our mission.

To my mom and brother David Alaniz who I have seen little since being on the east coast.

To my family at Coronado Baptist, Mike Woods, Dan Dodge, Alan & Barb Spencer and Parents of Teens, Ricky & Sandra Pearson, Teresa & Jesse Shaw for the birth of Joshua, Bill & Laura Randag, Frank & Carolyn Stewart, Andrea & Brooks Danley, Soldiers Angels, Louie & Susan Saenz who for the past two years inspired me to read and gave me books and CDs of different subjects, and many others for prayers and care packages, Lisa Ritter for watching all the kids when I was gone, what a great help when we needed it. Also Craig and Dalene Hentzel.

Finally, to my wife and sons who I saw just a few times from January 2005 to May 2007. Your Sacrifice of being without a husband and father has been great. I love you all!

I want to Thank:

The Tafoya family: Fred & Carrie, Uncle Fred, Bobby, Richard, Cynthia, Becky, Linda, Paul, Pat, Tommy, Andy Tiger, Angie, uncles and aunts and cousins.

Ken Craft, Bryan & Michelle McCrea, Rich and Maryanne Molton, Paul Clementi, Coach Martinez of Ventura High School, Verna Torres, My college roommate Jon Mata.

My first CDR Leo "The Rio" Enright who was an inspiration when it came to running when in VF-11.

My Massidda family Joe & Joan, Charley & Dene, Bill & Mary, Scott & Michelle, Todd, and Alison, and the rest of the Massidda Clan.

Thank you Nat Edwards, John Ortiz, Paul Cunningham, Christopher Cavoli, and Jake Jacobson.

PURPOSE

The purpose of this account was in response to what I saw and did in Iraq. Through this inflection, I realize that I am responsible for everything that has been under my control both good and bad, it seems that the bad sometimes outweighs the good but it's what perspective you look through. In all actuality, we all have this problem. It is like an expert bowman who can hit a quarter with the tip of his arrow from over fifty feet away, which takes years of practice and dedication.

I heard of a similar illustration by a speaker named Jon Randals who recently impressed on my heart the reality of "Missing the Mark". This concept of hitting the "bullesye" and the center or goal will always be real to me.

It is amazing to hear of the many stories of the good that comes out of the reports from Afghanistan or Iraq but never makes it to prime time news. Why does this happen so much both in the US and overseas? I think it is a travesty to see all the good going on and the Soldiers doing their best to help others in others struggle for freedom that it gets pushed to a blog rather than front page news. This is why we are there! Fighting a two war front both in Afghanistan and Iraq tends to bury the meat of the story from the readers. How can we expect the American readers to really understand what is the situation overseas during wartime? I think this will continue to be an ongoing battle with the media, a lifetime of newspapers which are almost dinosaurs on the verge of extinction in the coming age, and the illiteracy of public concern with foreign events.

This is how the information gap and influence of all information has on each of us. It can be the difference between winning and losing an asymmetrical war or counterterrorism fight.

I think it is reasonable to say that information is the center of gravity for a modern or ancient army and has changed the way we are fighting wars today. As we learn more of the enemy and how he operates in any environment or culture whether in the humid jungles of some island or the desert where resources are scarce, he is always evolving. The enemy has adapted his tactics to our current threat as we have done the same. We have to be faster than his first move and anticipate his next move before he reacts.

While living in Iraq on an Iraqi Forward Observation Base (FOB), I began to learn the way of life, and the adapted lifestyle of my comrades. I found it many times lonely, the kind of loneliness that goes to the core of ones soul. What could satisfy my inner turmoil and pain that I saw on a daily basis? It goes deeper than the companionship of helping brothers on a mission or the touch of a woman's words to a mans ears. This is one of the reasons for the inspirational verses and quotes. I am reminded of the story of David when he was hiding from Saul in the mountains. Those mountains are actually large cliffs that oversee the Dead Sea in Israel. If you ever get a chance to visit Israel and go along the Dead Sea, along the mountains where they found the Dead Sea Scrolls, this is where David hid and escaped from Saul who was the acting king. This is what gave me the inspiration when I looked at how his life was always dealing with pain, grief, heartache, and it is encouraging for those that read it. This is why Psalm 119 was on my heart. There are many others but this happens to be the longest Psalm in the bible which I am still acquainting myself with.

When I added the other Tips of what Muslims may do and common courtesies, I was thinking of all the times I made mistakes when greeting someone, eating, or just listening to them speak. They are there to help those that are visiting other countries who may not be familiar with some of the customs and may find themselves into a predicament and not know why. They will be very useful to others as I have remembered those incidents in Iraq. Many times my interpreters saved me from peril because of the looseness of my lips.

I am convinced in my heart that it is necessary to help those as much as possible that I come into contact with. I recently spent some time at the El Paso Rescue Mission just listening to some of the men and women that were passing through the small sanctuary. There are many veterans that I spoke to there that had lost their way and couldn't find their path again. My heart went out to the ones that destroyed their lives. A friend of mine Robert who owns several Bagel Shops explained to me the importance of having a father and the impacts it makes on men's futures. He has a quote that says, "it is easier to Build a Boy than, to Mend a Man". There is so much truth to this statement in Iraq for young men that don't have fathers to teach them how to be a young man and I know Iraqi boys will need much prayer on how to become instrumental in the development of their country and their families. This is why Robert has dedicated his time for over 13 years in helping develop and mentor young men in El Paso. My hats off to Robert as he changes this town.

He reminds me of my cousins and uncles Ronnie and Ray Garcia, Tiger, Tommy, Andy, Paul, Pat Tafoya who has spent their lives giving back to the young boys of Ventura California. Many athletes came through their ranks as they coached football, wrestling, baseball, basketball, and other sports to help other boys become men. Again, "It is easier to Build a Boy than to Mend a Man."

Taking this journey and writing this book was one of the biggest steps I have ever taken. I had many long hours in struggling to get my heart onto paper. I don't want to be a prisoner in my own mind or fearful of the future. Fear will immobilize us and it is said that "Fear is the Thief of Dreams" and fear steals what you cherish in your heart. Freedom and Joy are wonderful and each of us is meant to experience those feelings on a daily basis. Live and enjoy your own personal journey of friendship and sacrifice.

When I was at the Information Operations Course in Kansas, I began to see other perspectives on how Information has influenced everything we do as Soldiers and individuals. Many respectable professors from Lincoln University came and spoke to us which gave us tremendous insight along the lines of Marketing, Anthropology, Education, and History of the ancient world. To them I am also thankful.

CHAPTER ONE

May I have another?

Coming Home

He stunk from not showering for weeks, but using those baby wipes every few hours to clean all the grime off his face stopped all the dirt from turning to mud from the constant sweat. Thank God for the makers of Baby Wipes! He was a constant giver of his time and was constantly reading books preparing for his second Masters Degree. Scott loved his work which meant evaluating young Air Defense Lieutenants of the 108th Brigade (BDE) at Fort Bliss on how to engage a Tactical Ballistic Missile (TBM) coming at you at Mach speed without vaporizing you or turning a clean pair of Michael Jordan's into a mud sandwich. I think the rest of the Fruit of the Loom guys would be happy they didn't have to sit in it too!

I waited patiently, as Scott and Cedrick, exited from the short bus ride from the airport and pulled into the now overflowing parking lot. Twenty hours earlier they were both flying from Kuwait along with the rest of the unit to El Paso. They were all happy to be home with their families or reunite with them soon. Scott passed me some Iraqi money with a picture of Saddam, a melted Hershey's bar, and other stuff as he shared stories of the First Marine Expeditionary Force (MEF) and how they rolled into Baghdad. I embraced him like a brother. We had already gone through hell together during Officer Candidate School

(OCS) and he even watched me change a used dressing in my leg that was filled with blood and pus. I had a hole about an inch deep from the Brown Recluse bite in which the Army wanted to amputate my left leg above the knee during the 14 week course a few years earlier. For the next thirty or so minutes, my ears listened intently as Scott and Cedrick, friends of mine, comrades, brothers, shared stories of fear and glory. I admit I was envious and jealous because I didn't get to go with the rest of the train to Baghdad. Yeah I deployed, but I didn't consider Saudi Arabia a place where the action was. **Inspiration Verse** Psalm 119:1 "Blessed are they whose ways are blameless, who walk according to the law of the LORD."

Getting To Baghdad On My Own

In my mind's eye, I saw myself running from mortars, bullets, with screaming all around as I imagined I was with them. I told them I would have gone with them, anything to be part of their experience. But it wouldn't happen, not in my lifetime, so I thought. I made up my mind then and there that I would somehow deploy to Baghdad. If it wasn't with a PATRIOT unit, then it would be somehow, someway, but I would figure it out. It was not that I wanted to hurt others or use my weapon when I had to choose between him and me. It was as I remembered, to have that kind of loyalty to another American, another beating heart that depended on me and I on him. To give all that I had for my God and Country! That would be one of the most challenging years I have ever had.

The next time I saw Cedrick was about five years later. He told me he had talked to Scott about my experiences living in Taji. Obviously not a walk in the park! **Inspiration Verse** Psalm 119:7 "I will praise you with an upright heart as I learn your righteous laws."

Cooking with Cedric

I remember Cedric saying, "Remember when you said you wanted to go to Baghdad, It was not all like you thought it was, was it fool?" Those words rang loud as we shared a steak at my house during his short visit to El Paso. The steak was undercooked but the conversation was on point. How do you undercook a steak? If you like it still moving, that is undercooked. If you like it medium done, that is the best kind. Cedrick had been in the Marines and Army and had been around the block when it came to tactics. It was peaceful to have someone to talk to. This is where my journey begins.

The Innovator Charles Taylor

One could feel almost threatened as if purpose in this life was diminished or had no effect. As for me and being useful to the War on Terror, that is how I felt at this point in my life. Charles Taylor probably thought this many times as he saw what his hands had created over a lifetime, literally fly by him. As a young man, he was very handy and smart at building bicycles and working with metal and engines. When the two brothers asked him to build an engine that could take their plane into flight, he did this beyond their expectations. When the glider made the historic flight from coast to coast, it literally crashed and broke almost every day.

He would spend hours fixing and repairing the plane every night for the next day. He was never given the opportunity to fly the plane, maybe it was because they were scared or nervous they he would take their ideas. Despite being close friends to the brothers, it may have been for many reasons. He would never see the rewards for his deeds. He died with no money in a hospital in his late 80's. Although he may have felt like a complete failure during his lifetime, many others considered his works and achievements some of the greatest in aviation history. The Charles Taylor Award is given to those individuals that have spent fifty years of their lives as mechanics or repairmen in the aviation field. Despite all of his accomplishments to the Wright Brothers, he never received any of their fame. It was because of him that there were so many breakthroughs in flying and its origins. Many have learned from Charles that there may be no tomorrow. That it may never come and we have to go and get what we want today. None of us want to live in the shadows of our failures of regret, that we did not achieve something when we had every opportunity to be successful no matter how little or grand the dream.

Like Charles, when we live with struggles that keep us from moving forward we die on the inside and the river within us becomes dry. I don't know why he died with nobody there and penniless, but I can guarantee that it had do to with something he did not resolve years earlier. It eventually ate at him like cancer and destroyed him. You can read more about his life on the internet and his Award at (http://en.wikipedia.org/wiki/Charlie_Taylor). **Inspiration Verse** Psalm 119:11 "I have hidden your word in my heart that I might not sin against you."

Afternoon at the Lake

It was my first day in Iraq in the long summer of 2006. There was a very loud "boom" as it shook the entire building where the rest of Team 0920 was assembled. We were receiving training on radios when we heard the large explosion. We all looked at each other with eyes wide open and said "Oh Man", we looked at each other and asked "was that what I think it was?" The noise of the explosion was so deafening as if it was right next to us. We walked out of the room which held all seven of us into the open bay and looked outside where the noise came from. I peeked through the fence to see a small hole and the remains of an 80 millimeter mortar round. I asked Suazo if this was going to be like this all the time. It was beginning to make sense to me really fast. There was someone out there who wanted me dead. Why did he want me dead? I never did anything to him! They got close that time, about 100 meters close, but today would NOT be their lucky day in killing me! The report of the incident was published at the next day's briefs and I was curious about the incident and what it said. You never know what is printed. I could get an honest answer from Ernie Suazo because he knows by firsthand experience wars expectations. He had been here before and it has affected him more on the outside than the inside. He doesn't like to take it from anybody.

Outside of the FOB (Forward Operating Base) Taji, just beyond the gates of Baghdad is where Team 0920 would set up our headquarters, except we lived on the Iraqi side. We didn't have much of an Alamo as some of the other MiT Teams had, but it was home. Other teams were off in a distant kind of away from the flagpole. For them it was a little quieter and peaceful without all the requirements of a brigade tactical operations center (TOC). Home for the rest of the 364 days in Iraq would be in the White House. Not every moment was a "Kung Fu" experience where I could imagine a cloud in my mind and recall the lessons of life from a bald headed monk who explained to me the mysteries of my inner self. But if I go back and rent the series at my neighborhood Blockbuster, those moments I suppose would be more "enlightening" to me as the youngest of the grasshoppers.

It was a short helicopter ride from Baghdad International the night before at about o'dark thirty in the morning that got us to Taji. We were greeted by smiling greensuiters that morning. They were smiling so much because they knew they only had ten more days in country before they were out of the sewage lake. I thought the lake was one in a million but recently a guy told me they had one also where he lived. Guess it wasn't the first of its kind and I wasn't Christopher Columbus from El Paso either. It was a sewage lake all around our area because Taji was the lowest place in the area and the Iraqi Army had no fuel to put in the pumps to kick out the sewage. So, naturally, as they say, "It always flows down hill." The sewage would seep out of the broken pipes underground and fill up this particular area first. My first night in Baghdad had the most beautiful peaceful sunset behind me. It was beautiful, like being at the beach in Ventura California just without California, if that makes sense.

First day in Iraq

I had been all over the world before passing through the war torn beautiful country of Iraq. I had almost got my pocket picked in Spain right next to a cathedral by a group of gypsies, I had gotten on a camel at the pyramids, and filled the Holy Wailing Wall with my prayers. Egypt had a familiar ring in the country as I remember watching Anwar Sadat

Anwar Sadat Memorial

lose his life while sitting in my high school classroom. Very horrible day that was! I spent an afternoon on Iwo Jima remembering the men of the Second World War and it was very touching as well. The films in color and HD really bring it to life for me. I don't know how they got up that mountain through the volcanic sand but it was done on complete determination and fear. **Inspiration Verse** Psalm 119:15 "I meditate on your precepts and consider your ways."

It's What You Believe That Matters Most

When I think of the disciple Peter, and how he realized that his last moments on earth were to be seeing the same world as Jesus saw it on his cross, the guilt of dying the same way was so incredible and overwhelming to him. It was so moving emotionally to me that it is one of the most touching stories I have ever heard. Here was a man who was in prison and knew he would face death by beheading, stabbed, burnt, speared through, used as a torch, or just some crazy way that

Nero imagined. When the guard told him he would die by crucifixion, he chose to die inverted, or upside down because that is how the world saw Jesus. The people of the day didn't completely understand as to why He came to die, and that is how the world saw Jesus and his teachings, completely upside down!

Hotel California

We checked into our hotel which had all the luxuries of an Iraqi FOB. They were open bays with mattresses the Pharaoh himself used. I think my back touched the ground when I lied on the springs thus my current back pain. This was the first of my many back troubles while in Iraq. We had bottled water from the wonderful lake just outside. The water could be drunk at our leisure or used to push down the waste after getting off the toilet. An Interesting toilet system with just a hole in the ground. I admit I never saw that before but remembered seeing some of them in Korea. The same guys that decided to turn off the water in the fountains when Rome was burning was probably the same guys that lived here in Taji. What a coincidence.

Our job at the Phoenix Academy was to get a few weeks training of culture, meet the team we would be replacing, and get used to the food. Getting used to the food had some difficulties at first because the pink stuff wouldn't do the trick. No matter what I did, the Montezuma's Revenge or Saddam's Revenge didn't get better with time. It would take a strong kick in the rear by a Superman punch to overcome this one. CIPRO and I became close friends. Closer than a brother! If David and Jonathon could be closer than a brother, than the pink stuff and me would be even closer! Getting used to the food I thought meant being able to eat what was on the US FOB. I didn't know that by the initial sharing of food with the Iraqi army would be the beginning of many days and nights sitting around and enjoying each other's ideas, stories, pain, and food. Man I love food! Who would of thought that the sharing of food and chai would bring about the most and best in all of the Iraqi Army.

I couldn't figure out why I was constantly sweating, but I realized it was over 110 degrees and later 115, 125 degrees and continually going up in the afternoons. I wasn't used to that torture even when we were at Fort Hood or Kuwait for training. I would poke fun of the Air Force and Navy guys and gals that couldn't stand the heat at Fort Hood, but I realized I was just prideful. Being in the best service of the United States Military kind of does that to you. A prior Air Force Pilot Bill Randag would argue that not to be true!

I quickly learned that running around the perimeter wasn't always a thing that I needed to do ever since that first day on the Iraqi side. I had no idea we were going to be living with Iraqi's but it seemed to have its good and bad moments as I settled into it. I will explain those interesting and fun times later.

All of the time, I had someone I could trust who would watch my six when and if things were going to hell and a hand basket quick. Ernie and I had served together at Fort Bliss for a number of years and I was really excited he was going to be with me the entire time. We worked together before and going through two months of training at Fort Hood really made me trust him more. My heart's inward prayer before I left was that God would watch out for me and bring me home safely. I think that is the common prayer by everyone who arrives or just to bring me back in one piece. They say there are no atheists in war, but I found that to be false. There are many who are stuck in the middle of believing and denying and there are those that just want or have to shut it out just to get by with the horror of war. Not a fun place, I have been there! **Inspiration Verse** Psalm 119:17 "Do good to your servant, and I will live; I will obey your word."

Veteran Army SGT Ken Kendricks

Ken Kendricks was in a similar place of being somewhere he didn't necessarily want to but duty led him there. When he was a sergeant in the Second World War overseas, he lived in a hole in the ground just like us. At this one moment he was preparing his Honor Guard for a special visitor. When the visitor finished thanking the rest of the Honor Guard who was lined up with him, he came to thank SGT Kendricks for his duty as well. Noticing that SGT Kendricks was rather thin and ravished, the visitor asked SGT Kendricks if he could do anything for him. SGT Kendricks literally weighed 95 lbs because of dysentery and looked as if he needed a V8. SGT Kendricks had the opportunity to ask for anything just to see what could be scrounged up when everything was in shortage. It was like asking a genie in a bottle for that one wish. So, SGT Kendricks answered in his lightly covered southern accent if he could have any eggs if they were available. "I haven't had any fresh eggs since the war and I would love it if we could have some" he asked with extreme politeness. The next day there were fresh eggs at the camp for everyone and it lasted for the rest of the war.

If you could only have what you ask for, I think life could be both good and bad. After that request, that visitor died some miles up the road a few weeks later when his vehicle overturned. When I asked the now Mr. Kendricks who it was that visited the camp, he said, "that poor man was General Patton." Sitting in the position I was I could only be thankful for the lesson he gave me at that moment. As for the Division guys that we trained with at Hood, they later moved to Baghdad and the one thing they knew they had to eat everyday was "Fresh eggs." Thank you GEN Patton for your humor. **Inspiration Verse** Psalm 119:25 "I am laid low in the dust; preserve my life according to your word."

I decided to get some runs in the evening when it was cooler while at the Phoenix Academy or else I would dry up like the California raisin guy. California was hot at times in the beautiful mountains of the Ojai Valley where I also grew up, and traveling to Ventura on the city bus was fun because getting to the beach and playing in the surf was worth the 50 minute ride. I was mostly hot because I was a hefty 200 pounds and so was everyone else on my seven man team. The intelligence guy was the thinnest but he and I liked to eat and snack as well together. That is why I missed the Food Network so much! We were so big that four of us broke the "Trainer" at Camp Buehring in Kuwait. It was a "rollover" simulator that manned four Soldiers and prepared us for an actual HMMWV that would turn over in country. That was kind of cool but the rest of the guys didn't get to go on it because we maxed the weight limit. Call me tubby, tubby!

The Phoenix Academy was located on Camp Taji, on the Iraqi side and was a training site for incoming Military Transition Teams. It gave us cultural awareness and that kind of stuff. It turned out at the camp that they had internet, laundry, and hot chow. We were allowed the hot chow and internet for a short time if it was working. Stingy buggars!

Again, the chow took some getting used to not because it was bad, but because my stomach couldn't handle the water. It stemmed from an injury I received in Officer Candidate School a few years earlier. That Brown Recluse bite just above the boot line on the first day got so infected the doctors suggested cutting off my left leg. After my short protest while going asleep from the anesthesia, the doctor realized that an incision about an inch deep while pushing from my knee cap to my ankle would allow the puss out of my leg. Oh, did I forget to mention that my leg had doubled in size from the ankle to just above the knee. Not fun! It would take years to recover because I was septic. Thank God for modern medicine. **Inspiration Verse** Psalm 119:28 "My soul is weary with sorrow; strengthen me according to your word."

Torture Chambers

The Phoenix Academy turned out to be an Iraqi base prior to the war. They said the rebar on the ceilings is where they would sling up the ropes and use the rooms for torture. It gave me chills to think that I was sleeping where others used to be possibly tortured. It was probably just a scare tactic but regardless, it was eye opening. Later on my interpreters showed me actual rooms used for torture, so they thought? It kept me awake and alert at night. That is why I slept with my 9MM and M14 at my side like a good book. Even more so when I saw pictures of a Transition Team that had been overrun when they were in their compound. When I began to learn about my counterparts and their stories, it is difficult that possibly, maybe just one of them was responsible for many of the horrors that we saw on the television about Saddam and his loyalists. That part of the unknown is something that everyone always asks themselves. I would have to learn as much as possible about my counterparts, to include their sense of going beyond the normal line in the sand.

We stayed at the Phoenix Academy for some time before going over to meet our new team. This would be the beginning of one crazy ride. Before we left, we had met with General Casey as he spoke to several groups in a small theater talking about being the "Tip of the Spear". He reminded me of my father in law Joe but a tiny bit smaller. I was surprised he was taking the time to meet with us because the main effort for the

US was putting a lot of hope into the Military Transition Teams as "the" or "an" exit strategy. I am not sure if it worked for our team because it was so obvious we were so dysfunctional. It's like every American family. Anyone who thinks they grew up normal is just abnormal. Cause it abnormal to be normal. The contradiction suggests that everyone has a different experience growing up these days. Anyway, that was the big push during this time because the MiTTs could do a lot and get things done with less. The only problem was that integrating with Iraqis is merely a personal decision to let go of conflicts and set aside any biases of the other side. If you couldn't get past this small area as a leader, than it would be much harder to work as a coalition and with the Iraqi leadership. Some MiTTs didn't transition as well and some may have not got as much done but our team in actuality did a whole lot.

Inspiration Verse Psalm 119:31 "I hold fast to your statutes, O LORD; do not let me be put to shame."

In Conclusion

The Strategic Level of Information Operations continues to evolve into a coherent message which will be worked out at the highest levels of the United States Government. This strategy although evolving, has had significant impacts on how we fight at the Tactical Level. My Transition Team had an important mission which supported the Strategic Level of Information by supporting the legitimacy of the Iraqi Army, the Iraqi Police and the Government of Iraq as the Prime Ministers Ready Reserve in the 9th Division. Leaders and planners of Information strategize on how to complete that mission and saw Military Transition Teams as the Tip of the Spear as said by General Casey when he briefed us at the small cinema on the Iraqi FOB in Taji.

CHAPTER TWO

June Bug or just an itch?

We rolled across the street in Nissan trucks and funny little jeeps. The little jeeps were Russian Jeeps that Iraqis had and they were called the "WaZ". I don't know the meaning but they sure did get a lot of looks when I drove on the US side. They were like driving in a small Jeep for kids. They were loud and had just the bare necessities for the drive. Comfort was really not an issue when planning to build these things. The old team set up our rooms on the second floor of a two storied building. The color was white and had yellow trim. It also had some trim that matched our little Maverick that we had in the 70's. That color was diarrhea green! Thank God for the colors of that generation. The entrance of our Headquarters or "Alamo" had a six foot wall with guards at the front of the entrance. This was the first time I've seen real Iraqi Army Soldiers. They looked malnourished but content. I don't know if they were smiling because they planned on skinning my head while I was sleeping or just getting me killed in the open while on patrol. My awareness quickly went up after just minutes there but through the next several months I realized they were on the same team. That gave me some comfort at night along with my Italian 9MM friend.

Family History

I heard several accounts of skinning or scalping when I grew up. Seeing all the movies of cowboys and Indians gives a little mind many impressionable things to build on. My family name is Tafoya which comes from Arizona where my family was from the Navaho Nation. I was first told that my great, great, great grandfather came to Mexico when he had a run in with several men. After killing the five men, he had to leave the area. He was a leader on the reservation there. Then my aunt Linda has done some research and she recently shared with me that there was probably not a whole lot of scalping going on over there. Nevertheless, I grew up going to Indian class while in elementary school and we discussed the great Navaho Nation as well as Chumash or other Indians that came. Everyone should have a chance to find out where their families come from as a child so it can build on your character. With all the limitations on schools and the subjects that they can be taught, it is probably outlawed today in public schools, who knows?

If Jericho's walls could speak

For the first time in my life it seemed as if I would be living inside a fortress. It was an armed fortress where guards with live AK-47s guarded the entrance. I wonder what my Iraqi friends thought as the US planes flew over their entrance during the war, scouting for live targets? Did they think that it would all come to an end or that the reports that "The US has not entered Baghdad" according to their Information Officer was true and they had nothing to fear? OK, it wasn't a fortress like we see in the old movies but it was with huge walls with guards looking over and peeking at those that wished to get into. Nevertheless, it was a fortress to me. There is a lot to imagine as if you were living in Jericho with an army at your doorstep waiting to get you, and kill you. It sends an eerie feeling through my spine when I begin to think about it more in detail. The thought of loud trumpets sounding and marching for seven days before my world as I knew it came down before me. It was such a horrifying moment that men turned white and became lifeless as the impenetrable walls came down. **Inspiration Verse** Psalm 119:35 "Direct me in the path of your commands, for there I find delight."

The wall had a side entrance where my US team would walk through and the other was the Iraqi entrance. There were several nice Toyota's for the Iraqi Colonel who ran the joint. He was head of the 2nd Brigade, 9th Division Iraqi Army Tank unit. A rather jolly man that resembled

Jackie Gleason but with a jump suit and thick mustache that he had from the 70's. He would soon become General and was very interesting when he would share stories of the war when he ate. He used to say, "you Americans do not play fair, you used airplanes in the war to destroy my battalion of T-72s (Russian tank) in about thirty minutes. "Not fair!" Not fair" in his thick accent. This Brigade was going through the ramp up phase and was in serious need of training and certification. Our job, if we were willing to accept it would be to ensure they could fight and be instrumental in the fight against Al Qaeda or other Anti Iraqi forces. This picture shows the front of our housing area which consisted of sewage and water, trash, and lots of mud and traffic. An amusing place to be!

The White House

We sat in briefs from other units on intelligence that seemed like forever teaching us about what was going on in the area just North of Baghdad. We were escorted, pulled on, and dragged around for ten days before we took over the reins for the old-team. Getting a place to sleep at night would be my highlight for that time. I happened to share a room with another captain before getting my own room. It wasn't much but I made it home. On the second floor was a patio and chairs in which we later made a pit for a camp fire and hung our US Flag for everyone on the Iraqi side to see. I admit we got a lot of dirty looks while we had it up. We were told later to remove our flag because it wasn't our country. Not fair! I later used this patio as a source of giving and friendship with our Iraqi counterparts and interpreters who lived with us. This is how I got the title of the book. **Inspiration Verse** Psalm 119:36 "Turn my heart toward your statutes and not toward selfish gain."

Living in the White House

There were no microphones in the front or a nice green lawn where helicopters could land but it was home. The building was made of long hallways in a U shape and rooms on each side. There were about a hundred Iraqi Officers and Soldiers that lived there along with Team 0920 and augmentees from 4th ID to support us with the vehicles and a Personal Support Detachment (PSD). There was no running water or toilets in the building. We had to use an outhouse outside and a shower trailer that looked like it was the worst we could scrounge up in all of Iraq. Oh by the way, the showers only worked when we had fuel and that was a problem for the first six months. If not having a shower didn't kill me, neither did the water that was used because it came from the Tigris River or Khark water treatment plant. Regardless, I have three arms now and nobody can tell me why? Even the doctor on the way out of Taji didn't believe me when I told him of the water we used. When you live with all the luxuries of war, it is hard to imagine anything less! That is where we lived for 365 days but it wasn't his fault.

In the morning there was the smell of hot tea and warm sewage. They both went hand and hand in Taji. The tea was filled with more sugar than water but that is not what bothered me cause I too have a sweet tooth. It was that the Iraqi host would just rinse out a cup or give me one of the other cups from the other officers when he was finished with it. Again, CIPRO became my good friend. I know of several stories in the New Testament where men and women sacrificed their stomachs for spreading their message. Many of the disciples had to go out and meet new and strange peoples and eat their food. They tried pig and shell fish that they had never eaten before because it was forbidden, but they tried it. I know they got sick at times but they were always thankful for what was put before them and they thanked God for His blessing. I made a point to thank God for the hospitality and say that prayer before I ate or drank my doom. Again, CIPRO and I became good friends. **Inspiration Verse** Psalm 119:37 "Turn my eyes away from worthless things; preserve my life according to your word."

A good interpreter will save your life!

We were introduced to our interpreters who would serve us by translating for Iraqi Soldiers, other Iraqi guests, and being on the economy when we were on a mission. Some came and gone but the ones that stayed turned out to be loyal teammates in whom I trusted and gained enormous respect for. They were in a position to support themselves by earning money for their personal needs and serve the US in freeing their country despite the enormous resentment from the community and political groups. Many risked their lives every day by leaving the FOB and returning the next day. It was a very sad day when we lost our first interpreter just four months into our tour in mid August 2006. David will be remembered as giving his life for us and we are in debt to him and his work. The other interpreters who I will change their names were also very special and I hated saying goodbye when I left. **Inspiration Verse** Psalm 119:38 "Fulfill your promise to your servant, so that you may be feared."

I would sit with the Iraqi Officers this first week in their TOC (Tactical Operations Cell) Headquarters and sip chai and watch Iraqi television of what was going on in the world and in Baghdad. The officers would smile and point at the TV as if it were their prized possession. Coincidentally it was. Cause as it was explained to me by the Brigade S3-Operations Offier, LTC A that they never had television when Saddam was in power. They didn't have much of anything because Saddam had it all they said. I wasn't sure what to believe but it started making a case for understanding that the Iraqi people were going to be identifying with what they knew before in their culture and they would be redefining it again after years of tyranny.

Who can imagine building and putting back together a culture, a way of life, a way of doing things for over thousands of years? I find it heartbreaking and discouraging to see so much destruction day in and day out. When you hear the explosions and shootings everyday just outside your window, life becomes very fragile, I mean cynicism and a negative perspective on life is probably the norm. It doesn't matter what your faith is, anyone that has lived in fear, being paralyzed by its horror will see that moving into a framework of cooperation with those that destroyed your way of life is not easy.

Each person had a story to tell. It was their brother, mother, cousin, friend, wife, or someone that was tortured or killed during the Saddam reign of terror. I tried to listen as much as possible to everyone's story and try to empathize with what they were going through. It is difficult to see the pain and anguish of a people that are going through the exodus of a new era. Much of it was associated with pain and horrible memories. The good memories are filled with hope for a new generation. Our interpreters were part of that new era as they raised their children in a crazy world and trusted for their families safety while they were earning a living. It is easy to be thankful for what you have after seeing my new friends and what they go through. But teaching those lessons to a new generation would be far from over. Forgetting those moments would also be easy when you live with every type of comfort imagined. So this is why I write, so I won't forget!

I experienced this while being in South Korea some years ago in 2005. Many men and women that live close to the Demilitarized Zone (DMZ) or in Seoul were very familiar with what went on in the 50s. The movement of North Korean troops through the DMZ and into Seoul was an amazing feat. They demolished the South Korean forces and quickly made their way down past Osan with heavy fighting. Although the North Korean Army did not get all the way to the southern peninsula where the water meets the port, their effects were felt throughout the country. It is interesting to say that those in Seoul and Osan remember the dreadfulness and share of the goodness of the US and the Soldiers that saved their lives. It was this push that kept the North Koreans from completely taking over the country. What is astounding is that down South, even as high as Taegu, the resentment for the US is very visible. They were not able to see the destruction of what went on up North as much as the people in Seoul saw and feel completely different about what the US did in the war. Many are filled with resentment and frankly are not ashamed to tell you this.

New Kids on the Block

When I was greeted by Lieutenant Colonel A, he had a slight grin matched to a very short haircut. He was only about five four but had a thickness to him as if he used to workout with weights. He wore some ribbons on his uniform and was very discreet. You could tell when he entered the room and began talking to Soldiers, his Soldiers listened with respect and were genuinely interested in his wisdom. The other S3 (operations officer) had been replaced because he just couldn't do the job. Very comical man at first but I learned later that he was all about himself. He would ask, "Alaniz, bring me some ice cream, You Americans have so much you don't need it all." I still laugh to myself when I think of him. **(TIP 1: Never call an Iraqi on a lie. It is very disrespectful and embarrassing especially in front of others. If they wanted to do something for you and could not fulfill the obligation, it was in their heart but not made possible for whatever reasons, so don't call them out).**

It was true we had lots of ice and ice cream but it wasn't for him because he never gave it to his soldiers. LTC A was kind of like a Daniel in the Old Testament. He would pray diligently every day, five times a day and was very humble. His humbleness did not overshadow his understanding of the area and overall perspective of the war. He had been to a NATO school earlier in his career before the war and was instrumental in developing plans on the battlefield for me while working with me. He knew his craft and needed less of me as I learned this of him.

As the old MiT team began to show us the ropes, we began driving around Taji and meeting all of the coalition leaders. Then we went around to all the units and the old S3 introduced me as the Iraqi Army S3 Advisor. I was actually the Maneuver Advisor but it still equaled the S3. I think once you help in this position you get wrapped up into it and is so busy of a job it never stopped. We were greeted at some places and fit right in and others didn't really care. I felt the need to be accepted and do our mission so I began coordination with these units in order to gain support for our team. It would be one of the biggest challenges. **Inspiration Verse** Psalm 119:39 "Take away the disgrace I dread, for your laws are good."

I wanted to do my best when replacing the old crew and made sure our work was noticed like the previous crew. It worked well for me in the past so why stop now from doing my best. I once told my Master Chief that I would work hard for him than any other person he had if he would just give me one day to prove it. I worked for 16 hours straight without sitting down or eating. He came to me at the end of the day and said in his Pilipino tone, "Alaniz, you got-ta jobe." I later became in charge of the officer wardroom seating 120 sailors while on the USS Forrestal and served many dignitaries and officials. Those were my squid days. I am in the middle.

Serving Crew USS Forrestal

The major took me around the camp, showed me what I needed to do and then after just a few days, I was doing the briefs. Man did it get busy. It turned out to be 6 meetings a day on the busiest of months. Before I knew it, we were in the Left Seat Ride of the Transfer of Authority (TOA) phase. The first five days was the Right Seat Ride where I sat and watched him do everything, then I was doing the driving and it piled on fast. Our first battlefield circulation we did right away in which we would drive around the entire Area of Operations (AO) and check on the Iraqi Army as well as gain situational awareness (SA) of the lay of the land. I needed a good night sleep because tomorrow was going to be an eye-opener.

We rolled out of the Iraqi FOB and took a stroll along the Tigris River, largely inhabited by the remnants of the Baathist party of Saddam Hussein. There were many palm trees along the river along with little children playing in the street with soccer balls and toys. Farmers and merchants also lined the sides of the road with their goods either waving or using their cell phones when we drove by. Later, I would experience one of the loudest noises I ever heard on this road as my convoy hit an IED. If there were children and people out, then the road was relatively safe, if there were no children or people, things were going to happen. **Inspiration Verse** Psalm 119:41-42 "May your unfailing love come to me, O LORD, your salvation according to your promise; then I will answer the one who taunts me, for I trust in your word."

Ventura Highway

The land was beautiful in my eyes and reminded me of Ventura California where I grew up because I could smell the eucalyptus trees and see palms from my side and rear window on my up-armored HMMWV. We went all around the area as far south as Rustamiyah in Baghdad and the Khark Water Treatment Plant to the north of us. That road north of us was littered with four feet holes because of IEDs laid on the road by insurgents. To my surprise, there were some of our Iraqi tanks just sitting at a checkpoint. Kind of scary to think that a couple of guys could hold off a platoon of enemy but they were there day and night. Those Iraqis and their presence kept the insurgents from hitting Taji hard with mortars and it was a dangerous road.

When we pulled back to the main route going north, which was the main road going from Baghdad to Balad, I got my bearing straight. This road traveled right next to Taji and had many markets and illegal sale points of gasoline in front of the main gate. When we pulled up to the checkpoint, there were many Iraqi soldiers walking around the outside area as if something had happened. I could tell, but I didn't know what. There was a heightened sense that something happened by the expressions of some of the soldiers but many others in the Iraqi Army didn't seem as if it was terribly urgent. It happened that we pulled up next to a T-72 (Russian Tank) and I began to see that there was nobody manning the gun. It seemed a bit odd but as I took a deeper look at the left side of the turret, there was a pool of blood on the side of the tank. Then I saw an Iraqi soldier kneeling in front of the tank. I began to take a knee and asked if there was an issue still. The Iraqi soldier said to my interpreter that a sniper had killed one of their soldiers just before we arrived. They had not cleared the area yet nor did it seem as if anyone had wanted to go and investigate the incident from about two hundred meters away. I thought to myself, why did nobody go and clear the area so they can all relax a bit and continue with their operational checkpoint? This was a part of understanding their fear and the unknown. It is difficult to move or breathe or even act when fear takes over. Getting through that part when it happens the first few times can mean being able to deal with fear in a good way. That is what I was seeing with my own two eyes. Fear had crippled this entire checkpoint and they needed leaders to direct and show them how to work through it. Leaders were hard to keep because everyone wanted to get by because of the current economic situation. Why get killed by being a hero when they could get a paycheck each month by just acting like a soldier is what was going through their minds. Dying won't pay for their kids or wives to live on or survive in the economy. So, if they don't take risks, they don't get killed!

Seeing the Blood on the Tank was an eye-opener

That was my first day out in battlespace. There would be many more like that in the year. I happened to pray a little prayer that went something like "Lord, don't let me lose my head today" and then I got back in the vehicle and we rolled back to camp. When we returned to camp, my Iraqi boss told us that they had lost about 50 soldiers so far that had been kidnapped and killed when they got off of duty and left the base for leave. Their leave was a bit different from ours as they pulled three weeks on and one week off. This didn't make sense. I was doing a full time job and they had time off, not fair at all.

Anyhow, these guys were getting into taxi cabs and then they were getting kidnapped. It was nothing like having our favorite taxi cab driver take us around when we needed a ride. It was a real problem that I was determined I would try to fix before I left country. I did just that. When I made a stink about the Iraqis getting time off in their own country, I was shocked when my boss gave me his opinion but I wanted them to get to work. My boss said they have to live with this and we get to leave, what is not fair about that? Plus, their contracts were that they joined an Army and those were their rules. They would get more than enough to handle as time went on. It was difficult to watch because some wouldn't come back to work by either being killed on patrol or quitting and just turning their weapons, clothes, and helmets to their leaders and walking away from their checkpoints. **Inspiration Verse** Psalm 119:45 "I will walk about in freedom, for I have sought out your precepts."

Where is the "N" in NEWS?

I would later experience in the deployment that when it came to reporting from our counterparts, information was neither timely nor accurate for first reports. You had to filter through the muck and find the truth. When reporting the incidents, it was coming from the North, East, West, and South geographically but not really accurate. When looking to the truth of the incidents, it was difficult for my Iraqi leadership to say the truth as known in their minds and put it into words. Their words may bind them to act or to sit on the information so they were careful on what they said.

The next week we said good bye to our replacements and signed for all of their gear and completed our Relief in Place, Transfer of Authority and gave them a ride to their new hooches before their plane picked them up. They seemed so happy and I couldn't blame them. It's hard not to be envious of others but I managed and looked forward to my time that I would be reunited with my wife and three boys. Matthew was the oldest of the three and he was special because he was my firstborn. I had the opportunity to bring him into this world and pulled him out of the womb because we had a midwife there in Georgia. Neat experience but

I don't want to do that again. Next time, I will watch it on the Discovery Channel.

We liked the name Matthew and I think it has more special meaning to me because of the first book in the New Testament. I am proud of him in so many ways. Joshua was a different story because he was about four months old when I first saw him because I was stationed in Saudi Arabia at the time on a Patriot Site getting ready for the invasion.

Saudi Arabia

Andrew, I missed in my heart the most because he was a month old when I left for Korea to work in Yongsan and then I got this job so it was about two and a half years that I had been away from him. I admit he gave me some strange looks when I got off the plane on leave and returned from Iraq. He gave me that "what chu talking about Willis" look? He actually klinged to my wifes legs and tried to hide under her as I said hello to all my children in the airport. **Inspiration Verse** Psalm 119:50 "My comfort in my suffering is this: Your promise preserves my life."

Now the mission was ours and our LTC could begin his way of doing things. He was not a loud person but very observant. He would watch and smile as did someone who knew all the answers. He spent some time with the Kurds and seemed to know everything about our mission. I really liked how he could go into any meeting and know what to say and get his point across without stumbling. He sounded like he had been here already. Many times I disliked his decisions but I knew he had his reasons and it seemed to make sense as time went on.

That next day we went out and it was kind of like a new ride because we were officially on our own. We left out of the back gate and went along the Tigris again. It was a calm day and the weather was beautiful. The homes had been built with the money from many of the leadership of the Baathist party and many who lived here were in Saddam's leadership. As we drove down the windy road, we came across another unit that had cordoned off the area in front of us about 500 meters in front of us. They quickly asked for our help and we supported this other unit to be the rear cordon on the north side while they protected the south. They were in a high pursuit chase when the chased vehicle ran into a telephone pole.

What was important at this time was not to be outdone or outwitted. At any point the enemy can slip by you and come and get you from behind. This can be very dangerous on the battlefield. If the enemy were to "En Passant" or pass by me without me knowing he could win the advantage. In chess, when an opponent moves his pawn next to yours, you have to opportunity to capture that piece on the next move by "En Passant" and move behind it. It is a clever move by the experienced and executed on an inexperienced player. I was certain I didn't want anyone sneaking up behind me. This is why we cordoned off the area for the other unit.

In front of us was a four door vehicle in which the driver had kidnapped two girls and was running from the police. The American HMMWV was a bit slower because it was bigger and weighed down because of the armor and they couldn't catch it. The small vehicle had lost control and hit a telephone pole, destroying the vehicle so that it couldn't be driven anymore. It was totaled. Stan was always fearless. I saw it and have a picture of if somewhere and was a little bothered because we didn't have a description of the guy. If I saw a guy with blood on him or was sweating overwhelmingly, that may be a hint it was him.

Blake, Me, Biah

I was the navigator of this HMMWV and the middle one of our convoy. I jumped out with the rest of our team and we began looking for this guy. What was weird is that at anytime you can be hit by a sniper and it was a fear that would build and build over the remainder of the tour. There was a small creek to the right of our vehicles and we were constantly looking in there as Ernie provided over watch of our mission. The little kids began coming out and began asking what we were doing. I said get back, don't come over here. Get back and they smiled and looked on curiously. It was probably a joke to them or game called Who can make the US Guy mad? Many more people gathered at the rear of our vehicles and it kind of made me nervous. Again, I was still fresh to the area and didn't know what to expect. **Inspiration Verse** Psalm 119:51 "The arrogant mock me without restraint, but I do not turn from your law."

Combat Action Badges

It didn't take long for us to see some of the crazy stuff that war brings because there was always something going on in our area. Marlon was the first to get his combat action badge. He had to go to Rustamiyah for something and help the Division team and was on his way to Baghdad and his convoy was hit with and IED (Improvised Explosive Devise). He said it scared the snot out of him. I think he got his in the first month we were there. This was my foxhole for the upcoming months. I didn't volunteer for the missions but it was like a revolving

Giving Gifts

door. As soon as the other guy went on a mission, it was my turn again. Remember, there were only seven of us on a team. Our boss wanted to make sure we were pulling our weight, all 200 pounds of it. The other guys who were augmentees were made part of our team as soon as I stepped into the TOC. They are awesome.

Our team spent a lot of time doing site improvement. I mean it really smelled all the time and we wanted it to be a bit like home and something resembling things in the US. That would begin by cleaning up the junk around the front of the White House. There were old truck parts, scraps of metal and lots of junk. We later used a Mortar Tube that was shot through by an Apache gunship that the boss called in as a monument for the entrance of the White House. These bad guys were using mortars in a field and we could never catch them. When the boss finally waited for the perfect opportunity and snuck up on them, he called in air support and they shot a round right through the barrel, making it completely useless. It was a great shot by the pilot. I began to like the guys in the sky as they watched out over us. **Inspiration Verse** Psalm 119:54 "Your decrees are the theme of my song wherever I lodge". The boss took it as a trophy for the house. It was kind of like living in "The House" on Ultimate Fighter. There was always something going on, someone wrestling, someone with some drama. It never ended.

When we drove into the entrance of our hotel, what we called the White House, it stunk because there was a trash pile there on the right and it just happened to be there for a few days before someone would pick it up. Then the outhouses were right next to that and they were rough. I admit I never lived in the country and never had an outhouse, and Lord if it is in Your will, please make me never own an outhouse. If Bruno the trashman on Sesame Street came by every now and then, the place would be awesome. But he never came. Can PBS loan him to us for a bit?

Lessons of a Trashman

First of all, they are called biological engineers. Being one or a janitor is a highly skilled and patient job. Many don't realize that those that deal with trash and cleaning all day are some of the smartest people and most humble. My stepdad Tony was one for a while. He was a brilliant man. He once shared with me that he won a chess match against the Santa Barbara champion. This match lasted eight hours. This is my tribute to famous trash men.

- Oscar the Grouch lived in a trashcan his whole life and he had a contract on a hit TV show.
- Fred Sanford and Lamont who sold junk for a living. They were trash men with style.

- The inventor of the trash compactor so we can have more of it but packed neatly in our homes.
- Boy George who became a temporary trash man and did community service for a small incident.
- Carl the Janitor is the intellectual Janitor. "I am the eyes and ears of this institution"-Breakfast Club.

Honestly, here is a lesson you will never forget about being humble. This is taken from the Business of Life: Ten lessons in leadership from a Janitor website.

Ten Lessons in Leadership from a Janitor

Unknown to the cadets at the US Air Force Academy, their janitor William "Bill" Crawford was a Medal of Honor winner. While we cadets busied ourselves preparing for academic exams, athletic events, Saturday morning parades and room inspections, or never-ending leadership classes, Bill quietly moved about the squadron mopping and buffing floors, emptying trash cans, cleaning toilets, or just tidying up the mess 100 college-age kids can leave in a dormitory. Sadly, and for many years, few of us gave him much notice, rendering little more than a passing nod or throwing a curt, "G'morning" in his direction as we hurried off to our daily duties. Why? Perhaps it was because of the way he did his job-he always kept the squadron area spotlessly clean, even the toilets and showers gleamed. Frankly, he did his job so well, none of us had to notice or get involved. After all, cleaning toilets was his job, not ours. What happened when they learned the truth? Word spread like wildfire among the cadets that we had a hero in our midst-Mr. Crawford, our janitor, had won the Medal! Cadets who had once passed by Bill with hardly a glance, now greeted him with a smile and a respectful, "Good morning, Mr. Crawford." Those who had before left a mess for the "janitor" to clean up started taking it upon themselves to put things in order. Most cadets routinely stopped to talk to Bill throughout the day and we even began inviting him to our formal squadron functions. He'd show up dressed in a conservative dark suit and quietly talk to those who approached him, the only sign of his heroics being a simple blue, star-spangled lapel pin. Almost overnight, Bill went from being a simple fixture in our squadron to one of our teammates. This was taken from the "Ten Lessons in Leadership from a Janitor" website on the internet.

Being in the midst of heroes is not always what it seems. There are many heroes within the Iraqi Army that have given their lives without any reservations and someday they will be honored with full works. I recently watched a special on World War Two where Japanese pilots shared their stories how they killed US Soldiers while attacking Pearl Harbor. They described the duty to fight and destroy the enemy of the US Navy. I wondered how long it took for television to allow others that were enemies of the US to share their thoughts and feelings against America and other Americans tolerate it. I wondered how Americans that were still angry from that war listened to these old men tell their stories. I imagine before too long we will be watching stories of those Muslims that fought against us share their stories of how they too fought us. It seems that we can go as far back as WWII, Korea, Vietnam, Panama, and the Iraq War of all those that hate us. I just want to live in a world of peace but know it is a difficult journey.

When I sat down with many of these Iraqi Soldiers, many of them too did share their stories of their battles with the US and it reminded me of what I saw on television. I was listening to these men share how they felt when they fought against us. Some of their expectations of the US were misleading as they saw some of the SCI-FI films before the war. They asked me where my air condition unit was under my body armor. They asked me if I could jump up a wall, or look through my glasses so they can see through the walls like me. This went on and on for some time before sharing with them that it was just movies and not real. They had seen so many Schwarzenegger and Alien films that they actually believed this. It would be nice to tell Governor Schwarzenegger that he played an important role in the deceiving of the Iraqis in the Gulf War and it wasn't just his muscles.

It is always good to have the Golden Rule on your side. I say this because I am constantly learning what it means to be the same person at work and treat others with respect as I am at home. It is a lesson that keeps on giving.

When We Were Soldiers-Iraqi Style

On the opposite right side was the front entrance where the vehicles came in. There were two Iraqi soldiers that sat in a little box that got about 4000 degrees in the summer. They would just sit there and sweat with small smiles. Sweat, sweat and continue to sweat. Eventually their clothes would just hang off of them. When the Iraqi leadership had guests, they would put on these neckerchiefs like Mel Gibson in "When We Were Soldiers" famous movie. When I was in OCS, they were filming that movie across the street from our barracks and we had to give up our neckerchiefs for Mel and his cast so they could finish their movie. I

Gate Guards

should have got royalties for using that in their film. I don't think they looked as good as us. I will save my OCS graduation picture for another time.

Well, these guys wore bright red ones like some flashy Las Vegas piano player I remember growing up. It looked so out of place because one day they would wear red berets, blue, purple, black, and they began to remind me of the Smurfs. When they wore the purple ones some guys would began to sing "Purple Rain". **Inspiration Verse** Psalm 119:55 "In the night I remember your name, O LORD, and I will keep your law".

The Iraqi COL whose name I will leave out because of his safety was a very giving person as well. This is when I began to sit in his presence and listen to his requests with my boss. When I began learning Arabic and doing some speaking, he thought it was entertaining and wanted me to attend his afternoon lunches. I didn't object and it was quite nice. If you were to go into the kitchen and see how the cook was preparing the meals, you would have never ate there as a respectable restaurant. I didn't' have a choice. So I didn't go into the kitchen for a while.

Cops are good at knowing what places to eat at because they always go through the back door. Ask a cop where the cleanest places to eat are. You'll be surprised they are not donut shops! This is my shout out for the cops. After the meals, the Iraqi COL would offer us a banana or "Moze" in Arabic. It was a neat custom. We spent many afternoons talking tactics of tanks and the war. Again, he was funny when he said that the US planes destroyed his battalion in less than ½ an hour. He had this TV that got satellite and he would watch the news with us in Arabic and would laugh out loud and smile while we read the words at the bottom. (**TIP 2: Never show the bottom of your feet to a Muslim when sitting. The foot is considered one of the most dirtiest parts of the body and is very disrespectful).**

The building also housed the infamous S2, COL J. He was a crook to the core. He would take confiscated vehicles from illegal checkpoints and sell them on the economy. We could never prove he was into kidnapping but his cell phone was always busy. He was very smart but very illegal. In some ways how could you blame them? They were used to hoarding things while Saddam was in power. I once pulled my weapon on him and almost shot him for stealing Ernie's knife. They were given to us while we were in training and Ernie used to brag about it. He got this one from Marlon (our S4) as he lost his first one. He was always losing stuff. We later got the S2 fired and then he got a better job at the division in Baghdad. It was because he had evil friends in high places. **Inspiration Verse** Psalm 119:57 "You are my portion, O LORD; I have promised to obey your words". We have to be careful about being ambitious and using what we have or to get more for selfish reasons.

The S4 was a calm and realistic person. He smiled frequently but not as a weakness but as if he knew how the system worked and he used it well. See, we had a certain amount of moneys that we gave the Iraqis to purchase the things they needed to become independent and ready for war. This is why he was always happy. If you didn't have money, he would ask when it was coming and then come see you when you got it. I think he later went to Egypt with some of his money. He had influence as well because he could get what his boss needed. The head boss and him were both COLs but there was only one in charge. Neat system but not like ours in many ways. They were off the British Army system and this is what they relied on to get them back to a fighting force. We had to show them how we fight so they could be successful at counter insurgency.

The S6 or communications officer was completely useless but funny. Never saw him except when there was food or he needed something. He used to tell me, "I was in prison for three years. Saddam didn't like me so he stuck me in a cell about three feet wide and just enough room so I could stand up." "Why did he do this to me" he would say. "I was a MiG pilot and was very good. Now I am the S6" as if completely satisfied with his progress.

At first the Iraqi Army had trouble getting people who were not associated with the Army to run the Army or the Government. Some of this was played out in the recent Blockbuster *Green Zone* with Matt Damon. That was impossible for them to keep corruption out of their system at that time and if you were of a different sect, that would make a difference as well. If you hated someone, you could claim an offense and someone who you paid could easily act as a witness against them. They were just trying to survive too! **Inspiration Verse** Psalm 119:63 "I am a friend to all who fear you, to all who follow your precepts."

If we walked out to the rear of the White House, there was an ammo storage area. There were more rounds in that area that could have blown me all the way back to the US, but for free. It already happened to an Ammo Holding Area in Baghdad while we were there. It made the evening news and scared the snot out of everyone because you could see and hear if for miles. This ammo area was contained by barb wire on top of large boxes filled with dirt and a constant guard. Then we had our wall that went around the white house but that would have made no difference. It could have destroyed a lot of things besides our building. When we (the US) conduct planning for ammunition, we calculate how much can be stored and regulate it very closely especially next to airfields. It was because the Iraqi army had nowhere to put it. Again, it goes back to the hording and the rules of engagement. They were not allowed to fire their guns and blow up houses except when we were not looking.

Hanging on "C" Block

There was also a little Iraqi jail outside. I found this when there was a soldier resting there that was caught for stealing. When they brought him to the Iraqi COL they were slapping him around and he had already been beaten up a bit. He was very happy when they stopped beating him and left him in that little jail outside. They called it Iraqi justice. As long as they didn't kill the guy I was straight and I didn't condone this either. To steal in their culture is very serious crime. If you got your right hand cut off for theft, you could only use your left hand. Well, they had a problem with using their left hand to shake or do things because that was the hand they used to clean their, well their bottoms. So, if you had to earn a living with one arm, and that was your left arm, well, it would be a little difficult, and nonetheless very shameful. So, lesson here is don't steal. It is a commandment! **Inspiration Verse** Psalm 119:65 "Do good to your servant according to your word, O LORD."

Just outside of the White House wall was the building generator. When it would run out of fuel, it was a comical scene. The building would go completely dark, but our generators located outside would kick in for our TOC (Tactical Operations Cell). The Iraqis would get very angry at the Headquarters Lieutenant. He was not very popular when the lights went out. When he would come and get yelled at, he would say, I don't have oil, or I don't have fuel. He would run around for the day and scrounge up some fuel or oil from the US or the Iraqi Army and then was told not to do this again. This happened a lot when we transitioned to not giving fuel to the Iraqi Army except we had to pay as well. When the US was tired of giving the fuel for the generator, many Iraqis would ask us if we were really as powerful as we say. They didn't understand that we had a limit and they needed to get their army and government working so they could be efficient.

It's a funny fallacy because some people use this illustration of power many times to prove their point. They say if God is so powerful and so mighty that he can make a rock so heavy and so big that He can't move it. There were 33 wrong answers on yahoo.com when I checked this. We must differentiate between Gods Will and his Power. Two different things! God is all powerful which there is no argument, He can do anything! The question is with His Will and whether He is willing to do something. Many get mad at God because he didn't stop some hurricane or allowed some horrible thing to take place. Believe me, God hurts when this happens but he allows it to happen because most of the time we don't want him in our business or ask when it's too late. Its kind of hard to blame God for that. Besides, the question is a fallacy anyway. Nice try.

Getting back to the fuel. This also ran the showers and then we would have to go to the US side for showers. A little inconvenience but we still had the outhouses. Nobody was in a hurry to take those from us. When the doo doo guy wouldn't show up and they were filled to the rim, the boss would give them some money to come save us from the overflow. Man that was gross. **(TIP 3: Never shake with the left hand because it is used for cleaning the body. This is considered very bad if offering your left hand. If you stole and had your right hand removed, it is a obvious social punishment. If you couldn't use or have your right hand, it would be difficult in life).**

Believe it or not, many of their problems had to do with water too. A simple case of athlete's foot would cripple an Iraqi soldier. A simple cut on the finger could get infected if not washed and cleaned properly. When I saw a guy that his foot smelled like rotten cheese, this could have been avoided if cleaned with proper soap and water. Despite having a hole in it where he said a Sniper shot him, he had other issues to deal with.

When I first saw Saddam's palace as we drove to Baghdad for our Iraqi COL to do some business, I thought to myself, man this guy had it all. The size of the door to the palace was ridiculous and well over 80 feet in length. The chair that I sat in was fit for a king. Who could live in such luxury? If you ever get a chance to visit the palace, do so and sit in the famous chair. On the other hand you might get ticked off at all the privates with NTVs (Non tactical Vehicles) driving around and everyone

In front of the Palace

having a good time. We had to struggle to get showers and these guys are eating ice cream and having a great time. What war were they fighting? Again, there are the have's and have not's. We were the have not's so I can't be bitter.

Saddam's Seat

Oh well, "Embrace the Suck" as MAJ Sonny Thompson says every now and then. This is where I saw an OCS classmate when I went to the palace. CPT Rob Ferrell I got to know a lot more at the Functional Area FA30 Information Operations Course. Good guy Rob is. It can't be great all the time so you got to embrace the times of pain.

In Conclusion.

Information Operations at the Operational Level is where we were operating there in Taji, Iraq. The Iraqi BDE was instrumental in conducting command and control of the units under the Iraq General's command. Trying to synchronize the US Information intent with the Iraqi Army Intent proved to be difficult at many times. It is very important to understand the culture and language of each country as an Information Officer. The use of language and understanding of each culture could have prevented so many difficulties that we continued to repeat over the year we were there. Dr. Larry Ross, Associate Professor of Sociology & Anthropology at Lincoln University made many distinctions of culture and spoke to the relevancy of understanding culture from the roots will help individuals in understanding each culture. He was very insightful and understands that there is much to be gained when you understand the origins of people and culture. Thank you Dr. Ross.

CHAPTER THREE

Angelina July

George Washington would be proud!

We began our missions immediately and conducted Combined and Joint operations outside the FOB of Taji. One of the first ones was Operation Cherry Tree. I have to change some of the names of the operations for obvious reasons of safety and intent of Iraqi Forces. There were a lot of trees outside the FOB on the main route from Baghdad to Balad that blocked the walls and vision of the towers. Since the Iraqi soldiers were very used to the area and knew the people, we would conduct a tree chop and meet the people.

Cherry
Chop

The base security had trouble seeing outside the gates and snipers were hitting the towers and we couldn't strike back right away because the view was blocked. This happened several times as someone would lay an IED outside on the road. Because there was so much traffic and civilians buying illegal gas, we had to do something. This was more successful than in Korea when the Soldiers at the Joint Security Area tried cutting down some trees that hindered the view from the South Korean side. Except nobody went crazy and used the axes to kill our Iraqi Soldiers. The Iraqis would have just shot them anyway because they didn't tip toe around when it came to protecting themselves. The Koreans also never heard of the Iraqi Death Blossom. If they gave you one, you couldn't put it in water. **Inspiration Verse** Psalm 119:66 "Teach me knowledge and good judgment, for I believe in your commands."

Not all of the locals were welcome in the area since this was a common illegal gas selling spot. There were a lot of bad guys in the area. Anyhow, the tree was cut and everyone was happy with the Iraqi Army, and the Police, and it helped get the bad guys out of the area. Except there was this one little problem. This particular restaurant or shop had been shot up several times and these guys just wanted to eat their lunch in the daytime. Your forces (Iraqi) let the bad guys come and cause havoc in the night when we are gone they said. Our Iraqi boss told them later "they couldn't have their chai and weapons too" which made for interesting conversations and shootouts like the old west.

Unhappy Cafe eaters

39

Spring Cleaning at the White House

July was also a time for us to continue to get to know the land and knowing every area to include canals, dirt roads, and possible trouble points. We drove in our up armored HMMWVs around the entire battlefield many times and our senior leader learned just about every spot like he lived there before. I know I had some issues with him but he was really a very impressive boss. When I look back, I wouldn't trade him for any other leader. He was that good but still stubborn. He wanted us to know the leaders that directly influenced the locals and had positive and negative influence on the events of the day. It was also a time of intense fighting. We had an Iraqi checkpoint that had been hit by a mortar along the Tigris and did some slight damage to one of the vehicles. On top of that I saw my first Iraqi Police Call. In the US we usually would get a lot of people or Soldiers together after an event and get a body's distance apart in a straight line. Your job was to stay in a straight line and walk looking down, looking for stuff, trash, or items on the ground so the area could be clean. This is why it was called a "Police Call" because we would arrest any trash that was parked illegally.

When we were at that checkpoint, Iraqi's were just throwing all the trash over the Texas "T" Barriers. I sat in my HMMWV and looked through the window and couldn't stop laughing at the comical site. It was very funny because they saw me and started laughing too. What was so gross is that the smell would just be blown back over the wall and it was like a fish dump that attracted every feline in the area to the smell. It smelled like the side a large vessel where all of the trash was gathered before throwing it into the ocean. It would stay there for sometimes weeks before making it into the ocean. Most people not familiar with going to sea have not experienced all the trash being thrown overboard and having to shovel it off or throw it into the large waves. A ship has to be 50 miles out or in international waters before dumping. I remember a few years ago, there were many hypodermic needles that washed up on the beach. This is because the tides brought it in and they were suspected of dumping in US waters. **Inspiration Verse** Psalm 119:67 "Before I was afflicted I went astray, but now I obey your word."

Trouble in the Tigris

July was also the month that I really began to understand the depths of how cruel and evil those that had no conscience or morals stooped to the lowest of all creation. We were told that men had gathered along the historic river of the Tigris and would kill individuals and push them out to the moving river to be found downstream. I witnessed this firsthand when a man who was about to be killed had escaped from the hands of these men and told us his story while dripping from the mirky water. There is so much history in that river and the people that lived there over the centuries that I refused to see it as just a single incident.

You got to ask yourself what this fear does to the new generations that grow up in this type of warzone. Everyone is fighting for their lives from day to day. Looking at the comparison of young men growing up in the US, even in the worst places or cites, none can compare with the realities of violence, shootings and bombs going off in the city. Kidnappings and senseless killings in Iraq have compared to some of the worst killing in history. The impacts of children growing up without their fathers and positive role models will hurt this country for decades.

Just to have a father take their sons to the park and play soccer or throw a ball to him is something that we take for granted in the western world. We can do these activities daily without any type of fear of breaking a curfew set by the city, or having a bomb go off near people in any large or small city in the US. Society for Iraq will be built on completely different morals and standards than any other country living in peace.

What about the other countries that continue to have war for decades and the impact on their society and the relationship of men growing up without fathers and role models? The difference of having a son come sit on your lap, run your hand on his back, putting your hand on his head and looking into his eyes and telling him that you love him. Or sitting on the edge of his bed at night and sharing that he means more than anything in the world to you. Many boys will never have this and it will be replaced by a loving mother or uncle or brother. It is not the same no matter who the role model is. It has to come from the dad!

When looking back at the river scene, it was very disturbing when one man in particular was basically begging for his life at gun point. That was some young man's dad, a husband, a father, or he was an uncle, and he was a son. Our Iraqi boss told us that about 50 of his soldiers had been taken along the East Gate and it affected the morale and hearts of his soldiers. They were being hunted and killed for serving their country. Their country's independence, their revolution was being fought right in front of our eyes. It was a part of history that was being decided every moment. I spoke with Ross and several others about what I had suspected about certain individuals that were responsible for the killings and we both agreed and confirmed that these particular men were responsible for all of the killings. Ross agreed we should pursue it and we made a presentation for our boss and told our Iraqi boss of our learning's.

When we told our boss that we know who they were, he also concurred and wanted them stopped. We showed some of the other leaders some pictures and they were amazed, angered, and ecstatic that there might be a solution to this problem. I requested a Bradley Fighting Vehicle and HMMWV platoon from our sister squadron and we cordoned off the house according my plan. I took my Iraqi CPT with me and we sat down with this sheik in his house and requested the individuals over some chai.

Bradley Training

I was getting very familiar with the US Bradley Fighting Vehicles as we heard them move over and over in our area. Our sister unit had them and we did several missions with them in the day and night. I wanted to learn about it more and some of our Soldiers got one and showed us how to drive it. It was a great experience on how this beast of a machine operates. We spent the early afternoon one day training on the obstacle course with it. I love the vehicle. This picture is the one where I began training on my first Bradley. The presence of this monsterous vehicle and its enormous ability to destroy its enemies has the ability to persuade even the most strongest of wills that we were serious in what we did. This may have been successful in persuading the local sheik to tell us who was doing all of the killing on the river. Ultimately he was responsible whether he knew of the killings or not. It was his turf and so there is no discussion. (**TIP 4: When offered something to eat or drink, it is very impolite and could be disrespectful if not accepted. Laying your spoon on your tea cup horizontally is a sign you do not want any more tea.**)

The killings began to stop and slow down immediately on the west side of the Tigris. It seemed to just push the guys out of our area and move across the river where our interpreter lived. The local sheik was very interested in listening to our story of what was taking place in his area. I found him to be very interesting and compassionate as we sat drinking chai with just me, him, my Iraqi captain and interpreter. Learning what was on his mind and his love for his countrymen seemed to be the heart of the conversation. He described how he liked the children to play in the streets and play without any fear of being hurt. He shared the same dreams that I experience with my children on a daily basis.

I thought for sure that the meeting with the sheik would be a turn for us as we rode along the sheiks area when doing patrols and it really did begin to slow down quite a bit. I have some personal pictures of some children and their excitement when they came up to me and I gave them a soccer ball. You could see the joy and pure happiness as he ran away with that ball that sunny afternoon. It is amazing to see how good is being done in the midst of chaos. The truth is that good things that are done will always be stronger than those dark evil deeds. **Inspiration Verse** Psalm 119:68 "You are good, and what you do is good."

I have lived in El Paso for some time now. When I think of what I was going through, it reminds me in some cases like home. El Paso is very similar to the area of the Tigris. El Paso or "The Pass" for many years has been seen as kind of a short cut to the North. The mountains go from North to South and end in Juarez Mexico. The sky is completely split so that if you were on the West Side, you get these beautiful sunrises as the mountain makes such a striking contrast of light and shades of blue, yellow, and ambers. If on the East Side, you get an early sunrise and beautiful sunset. You really can't lose no matter what side you are on but I am kind of partial to the West Side because of the greenery of the land and the water along the upper valley.

Plus, if you like pizza, this is where you want to visit. There is a small restaurant in the Franklin shopping center right across from Blockbuster Video that has the most amazing pie. Artevino's has a thin crust pizza that doesn't weigh you down. I don't like feeling so full from the weight of the dough and this place really makes their crust just right. This is where I pigged out when I was on leave. Now with the economy being so bad, I resort to Wal Mart fresh pizzas. They are really good too!

We happened to be on patrol again and ran up on a scene along the Tigris where one of our battalion MiT Teams was operating. There was a very big explosion just minutes before where a vehicle was hit by an IED. The trigger man was in the bushes where we found the wire leading to a small lookout area. It was a very large hole. The attacks just seemed to increase when the summer months got hotter. CPT Lane was the officer that called us to the event.

He is a brave guy who was once shot in the chest and lived to tell his story. He had a bruise all over his white pasty chest and he said it was like getting hit by a baseball bat. I never been hit by a baseball bat but I have been hit by my brother David and, well that hurts pretty good. When he was shot, it threw him down into the turret of his HMMWV, but he got back up and started shooting his M240 and returned fire. He was hit square in the chest but thank God for body armor and Donald Rumsfeld. It seemed that the enemy was very conscious of what we were doing and making preparations for us every time we went down that road. It is not difficult to hear a T-72 or BMP come down the road because there is so much smoke, the tracks on the road, and the huge engine. In the dessert, that wouldn't have mattered so much. But when you only have one road to travel on, then you are a bit limited.

Lost in the Desert

I had my share of hanging out in the dessert outside Tobin Wells in El Paso. The first time out in the dessert in 2001 was a very humbling experience. I was supposed to go out with another lieutenant and do a recon of the area. Well, the lieutenant left me so I had to do it on my own. I never been out in the dessert so I grabbed my jeep and headed out to the dessert with a map, compass, water, and protein bar. I got a flat and couldn't find the lock for the tire. I was riding on a rim for miles. I finally found a road and then went to a junk yard to get a tire. It was a $400 dollar three hour tour. Lesson learned: don't go by yourself to the dessert. Recently a UFC fighter Evan Tanner, whom I loved to watch died when his motorcycle ran out of gas in the mountains and he had no water. It was a very sad day for the Ultimate Fighting Championship.

Things that are normal in the western world are not in Iraq. The Iraqi soldiers that we lived with like to wrestle and knew some martial arts but were not very good because they learned from the movies. Without serious training and discipline, an individual will never be able to use those skills when it mattered most. I liked to wrestle some of the guys and practice martial arts with them. Some thought that the type of fighting that was considered cage fighting didn't catch on professionally for them in Iraq and was difficult to make a living on. They just dealt with this war every single day. I suppose sometime in the future when there is peace, they will have fighting gyms and wrestling and other martial arts gyms. If they can have shows like "Iraqi Idol" than it will take some time as well for them to move forward.

The kind of patrols we did were done at all times of the day and night. One afternoon we conducted a patrol on our southern boundary because there was a lot of fighting in the evenings and people were afraid of the insurgents in the area at night. The people were very generous as we arrived. You never know what kind of greeting you will get when traveling. I prefer the one with an outstretched hand compared to flying metal and loud noises. We gave the children soccer balls and t-shirts that we stockpiled in our vehicles. It was an attempt to "win the hearts and minds" as I later recalled. It was amazing how our country had helped produce these products with Iraqi flags on the soccer balls and shirts. The local people there gave us hot chai and water from the canal that was dirty as I'll get, so I passed on this first one. It was because all the floaties were huge in the glass. I didn't want to constantly look for a place to go to the bathroom while driving in our metal box or hunched over the toilet when we finished the patrol. We pulled away and continued on our mission. **Inspiration Verse** Psalm 119:71 "It was good for me to be afflicted so that I might learn your decrees."

Building an Honest Army

When looking at the Iraqi Army, there were many things that they needed again to be a powerful army. One area of concern was that the corruption needed to be under control, driven by a constant need of supplies and materials, adhering to discipline under fire within the ranks, they needed strict supervision. I compare it to the most important of all foundations. When cooking or making a stock, you need fresh vegetables and a love for cooking. Any stock just won't do. The French word "fond" or translated "foundation" as was told to me is the right recipe for success. Their beginning of a new army would not come quickly because it takes time and preparation to build an army. Anyone who does not see that important lesson is not very understanding of what it takes to be successful.

A funny thing about languages is that in some ways they all work together. If you take the word "conozko" in Spanish, it is the same as "kinosis" in Greek. If you take the word mom, "oma," "opa" (Korean), "mama", "papa", "papie" (Spanish), "abba" (Hebrew), and so on, they all sound very similar and mean mom and pop or daddy. That is the same for the Iraqi language and languages in general. It is the window of relationships. I spent many hours and late nights learning phrases and words to build those important relationships with our Iraqi comrades which proved to be very helpful for all of us.

Ordnance in the Canal

We ran into a dead end and began to look into a canal and its banks as we exited the vehicles. There was something odd about the area because the road had been blocked by a lot of debris and palms. Our NCOIC for the trip was SSG Moudry and my usual driver was SPC Burke but he was my dismount this day. They were in my HMMWV and we dismounted to get a better look while the other two vehicles provided over watch with their larger caliber weapons. Our smart guy Ross was with me and we began walking into the banks of the canal when Moudry called out that he saw a 155MM round at the bottom of the opposite side. He found about four while Ross and I found about six. A man who lived across the street who appeared to be studying our moves with obvious curiosity approached my team and told me how the large rounds made their way into the drying canal. He said during the war, a large Iraqi tank had been driving along the canal as US planes began attacking him. The tank members were throwing the rounds into the canal to avoid being destroyed by the US plane and blown to pieces. This is where we found them years later. It was another piece of time that had been untouched. As if a detective were putting the pieces to a crime scene together or brushing away the dust that covered the key to his unanswered questions. It had a very interesting ending and another great example of Air Superiority when US planes penetrated so deep into enemy territory that everyone was on the run. **(TIP 5: If there are lots of roadblocks, you're probably not wanted).** There were also many foxholes and sandbags on the other side of the canal. The enemy was getting ready for anyone that drove by at night. Luckily for us "We own the Night".

As we waited for over four hours for EOD (Explosive Ordnance Disposal) to destroy the rounds, we high fived it with one of our battalion MiT teams who owned the area so they could secure the area and take over the watch when EOD arrived. Our vehicles continued back to the FOB when Moudry saw a man with an AK and our first vehicle went to cordon off the far side. Moudry exited the HMMWV with lightning speed and me on his tail with other members in trail as we began chasing the man. We thought he went into a home and we cleared the home but couldn't find the weapon or the man. **(TIP 6:**

If you enter a home without the male of the household present or not invited, you will cause their home to be unclean or even make more enemies. The children will have every right to be angry at your uninvited presence). We thought he headed toward the other vehicle as he ran through the field.

A Cold Dark Night

I recall it being a very tense moment. I remember the story of waiting, quietly, not making a sound or even breathing to not give away their hiding place. The story of Anne Frank is a vivid description of hiding for fear of their lives. I can imagine the Iraqi families felt the horror and sheet terror as the Jews felt in their hiding places waiting to found. The stories of the killings and murdering of the Jews circulated and spread fear amongst those in hiding. I know the Iraqi people in that home must have felt sheer terror when we entered their home that afternoon.

Wives, children, and relatives that day probably asked themselves why were their husbands, dads, and heroes not there that day to see that we as US Soldiers did not enter their home without permission. These incidents that happened were always very difficult and we tried in our power to avoid scaring the children and families. What the media ends up showing in many circumstances is that the US Soldiers were excessively violent or not sympathetic in these situations. I would argue that many Soldiers are compassionate and have a heart for the people of Iraq and do their best to help them in every situation. Except there are those times when the situation is extremely fragile and stressful that something terrible happens. Thank God that nothing terrible ever happened to those in their homes that we entered. I am sure that those few times that those families will remember that incident and unfortunately make a negative conclusion about the treatment of their people. I would hope that most children and adults there in Iraq would not make their final conclusion on those difficult moments. We have done a lot for the people of Iraq and will continue to do until they have their nation free again.

Rollover, Rollover, Rollover

The first vehicle that Ross was in went over a small canal to head off the fugitive and quietly waited for the man to appear from our West. The man with the AK rifle could not be found so Ross's HMMWV went back over a very small canal and cut the edge too short and the vehicle began to fall in to the canal. I was just on the other side about 200 meters away to the east while the south was covered by the third vehicle. Within a matter of seconds I heard the first scariest sound of the time I was there in Iraq. Ross yelled "Rollover, Rollover, Rollover." From the previous months I thought I would never use or we would never use those words, but they rang out long and fast over the cracking radio. I stopped everything I was doing and yelled over the radio where they were. No Answer. I asked again from my driver and gunner and they didn't know because we lost sight of them for a moment over the six foot walls. They were right next to us according to our instruments. **Inspiration Verse** Psalm 119:74 "May those who fear you rejoice when they see me, for I have put my hope in your word."

I jumped out of my vehicle and ran to the canal and then, just over on the south side of the canal was a turned over HMMWV. In my field of vision was the bottom of the vehicle. I have never seen the bottom of a HMMWV and it was something that I was not prepared for. Usually vehicles rode on wheels and it didn't make sense. In my mind, all I could think about was that the gunner was dead or drowned or cut in half. The vehicle was submerged under water and I knew was filling fast. I was about 50 meters from the HMMWV and the first one there and I started peeling off my gear, my weapon, my Kevlar and left it at the base of the canal. I didn't care where I threw them at the time but should have been more careful as not to und up in someone else's hands to put a few rounds in my chest. An Iraqi man was pointing to the vehicle and was really scared for the Soldiers in the cab as I read the international facial expression of "help". The vehicle lay on its top and I jumped on the bottom of the overturned vehicle and with two steps made it to the back of the vehicle and jumped into the canal. Moudry made it there next and he jumped straight in feet first. We tried to pull the door open but it was stuck in the front and the back of that side. We were screaming to open the door and it finally creaked open and nothing prepared me for what I was about to see. When I pulled a Soldier out and then got a clear view of the gunners hatch, I thought for certain he would need serious medical treatment. I couldn't see the Soldier's body except his head which was sticking up out of the black water from his chin up. I quickly yelled if he was ok and he quickly said "I think so?" He looked like one of the people who lies on a magicians table who was about to be sawed in half, the part where you can only see his head. The others made it out of the other side except an interpreter. He was yelling at the top of his lungs and he couldn't move because he was pinned down. We constantly teased him because he was on the big boy diet. We had to cut him out of the seat with a knife and drag him out. He began to cry and shake and uncontrollably as I leaned him against a mud wall and slapped him. He was still shook up for days after. The guys in this picture were responsible for pointing to me and letting me know my guys were in trouble.

The men who helped

One of the personal lessons in this event is that the Iraqi people are wonderful people. They are kind and willing to help and they just want to have their freedom. They weren't concerned with what skin color we had or from what planet we came from, except that they wanted to see a potentially life threatening situation be avoided and preserve the life of the men inside the vehicle. I am grateful as well as the rest of my men. **Inspiration Verse** Psalm 119:76 "May your unfailing love be my comfort, according to your promise to your servant."

I knew our interpreter thought in his mind that he wasn't getting paid enough after that event. When the Iraqi S3 came out with a busted up eye, all I could do is laugh and say "I told you so". You see, I told him to keep his AK 47 pointed down just in case an event he could come out shooting. I even told him twice but in the end, he said I was right. He smashed his eye onto the tip of the weapon and busted up his brow pretty good. He was ok but it made for a good Iraqi bar story. (**TIP 7: Pointing weapons down in vehicles is one of the safest ways to travel. It is possible to be injured by the tip of the weapon penetrating soft tissue during crashes**). In the end, we all made it back to the FOB in the late evening with some scolding from the boss. This was an all day affair starting from about six that morning. We were smoked, we stunk, and we were starving. Some were a little dehydrated, We made it back so late because the vehicle had to get overturned and everything accounted for including weapons and radios. The tow truck came just before night fall. Thank God for the wrecker!

Our boss was of course really upset and started to yell at me when I called him. Ross never approached him about the incident from that point but of course I got the behind chewing. Not fun with my boss. It was ok for him but not for us to make mistakes. I think he was worried about who would fix the darn thing. We didn't have mechanics and parts to replace them so at times it was a little tense with the coalition fixing our stuff. Once when I asked to use the MWR facilities on the US FOB, they told me "no" because I was Iraqi. I wanted to smack that guy so hard but I yelled back and showed him the US Flag on my shoulder. I still couldn't use it that time because I lived with Iraqi's. There was just a little confusion from the guy at the front desk. They only follow orders so you can't shoot the messenger.

My Friend Manny

July continued to be a real Fourth of July like atmosphere. I snapped a picture of my friend Manny who was with me before in the Great state of Texas. It's a small army when you think you will never see people again, but then lookey lookey, Surprise! When the Iraqi Soldiers were starting to get injured a lot they would say "En Shallah" which translates "God willing". They didn't like it if we said it when they asked for stuff or things. They knew we had the ability to get "Stuff", but they insisted on using it when I asked them for the same type of favors. Ohhhh, and if you called them a liar or questioned their integrity, it was considered very disrespectful.

In Conclusion.

Information Operations at the Tactical Level is where the boots on the ground get the work done. This is where the themes and messages of the CDR really begin to take shape. It is where the Core Capabilities of Information Operation have effect and see almost immediate results as per Measures of Performance (MOPs) and Measures of Effectiveness (MOEs).

When observing different perspectives on Education and Information, I had observed and compared many of the issues that Iraq will be facing are very similar to the ones we currently face in the US with our children. Issues of resentment, abandonment, anger, feeling inadequate are just some of the many issues that teens grow up in the US will continue to deal with. There is an obvious need for intervention and understanding and Dr. Henry from Lincoln University had many interesting points of learning which is crucial in understanding culture. Realizing that environment can change behavior and understanding these correlations is necessary to understanding people in general. Within the realm of Information Operations we should engage aspects of the entire spectrum and synthesize what we have learned in order to benefit the CDR and the area of operations at the tactical level. Rather than be like my children's favorite television show *Sponge Bob*, we need to be like Joe Sponge and soak it all in!

General McCrystal made it very clear in the Information Operations war in Afghanistan that we must change our tactics and begin to look at the individual on the ground and what they go through daily. The difficulties of what it takes to grow crops, raise a family, and feed them all without getting killed by the Taliban is a battle in itself. The General knows that by blowing up ones house and causing extensive damage from a well placed missile from the sky can cause negative second and third order of effects on the operations environment. It is the tactical level at which the decisions of each Soldier must be in aligned with the CDR at the operational level. Understanding the tactical level of information Operations is also where we will begin to hone and become experts in our craft.

CHAPTER FOUR

Augustus

As the months passed and the weather got even hotter, I thought for sure it would slow down. By this time I had been going out two to four times a week and I was smoked. Not from going out on mission but because I had to still run the TOC when I got back. It didn't matter what time I got back. Plus I had to still go as the S3 to the many sister squadron and higher meetings. I was getting tired quickly. If I didn't slow down, I would get burnt out from my boss or the heat.

Operation Peg Leg (Internal Name)

Up north, we thought we had some allies from the Iraqis that guarded the Khark Water Treatment Plant but one guy tried setting an IED on the road and got all blown up and his leg, hence the name Operation Peg Leg. It wasn't necessary to block out his eyes on this one picture cause he did that himself. I removed this picture because of the gruesome horror of war. I don't think it is fitting for this guy who is burnt at his head, hands, and feet to be viewed. The way some do favors in the Iraqi Army is kind of complicating as I have figured out. They asked if we could go and pick him up from the Kadamiyah hospital and then transport him to an ambulance on our northern boundary so he could die with his family. And he was going to die! Well the operation went off without a hitch and all our guys came home safely. I must reiterate that I don't take any type of comfort, I am not vindictive, or celebrate the demise of another individual in any situation. I feel horribly bad because unless you walk in any man's shoes or in this case his "leg", you don't know why he did it or what he is going through. It is easy to throw the first stone, but I can guarantee if you come to a fight with a rock, the chances are, you are going to get hit with one back. Just ask my brother who shot me in the head with a .22 caliber pellet gun. My scar is still there on my forehead between my eyes. Anyways, someone will bring a blade, and another guy a gun, and it never stops.

One particular mission, I was linking up a team of Iraqis to conduct a joint mission with one of our US units on the FOB. When we drove over there through the checkpoint, it didn't occur to me that I would have any issues with this team. I mean nothing ever went wrong! As they followed my vehicle in a large truck that had steel plates on the sides to protect their soldiers, kind of a what our armor looked like when Soldiers in Kuwait started welding it to vehicles at the beginning of the war. So it was just about an hour before we were going to go and conduct the mission. When the soldiers got out of the truck and talking with me. I tried to ease their minds and tell them not to be scared. I started conducting some Pre Combat Checks and inspected their gear. They saw that I had a puzzled look on my face and asked through the interpreter what was wrong. I asked where was their food, and water, and bullets. They looked at each other and said what bullets? I said the bullets you will need to kill the enemy? They said what enemy? We are going to go and fight tonight? There were no batteries in their first generation Night Vision Goggles and they were a wreck. After closer inspection I realized they were just green recruits with a senior soldier. This was the kind of thing that would constantly go on.

On another occasion after moving all the tanks to our positions and getting all the soldiers there, the jundee came and asked me for fuel. I said for what? They actually did not bring enough fuel to drive the tanks back to the base. So they sat on the side of the road and had vendors come and bring them chai and food. How funny.

Being separated from family with occasional conversations with my true friends in the US and my wife in El Paso made it very lonesome there in Taji. I was getting lonely but I heard that a friend was coming from the US who was getting assigned to one of the battalions in our

Iraqi BDE. He was a good guy who I wanted to talk with and make sure he was gonna be safe. I will probably post this picture sometime in the future on my site. **Inspiration Verse** Psalm 119:77 "Let your compassion come to me that I may live, for your law is my delight."

Don't Say I didn't Warn You!

When they, that new team arrived for their in-brief from us, we told them no matter what they did that first day to be safe. We told them they were going to get IED'd, shot at, or RPGd when on their patrol. He thought I was crazy and just laughed and shrugged it off. They didn't believe me!

The radio cracked open wide as I sat there waiting for their report. Screams from grown men just dosen't set well with me and still bother me when I hear them. The radio was thick with chatter and as far as I could tell from the initial report, they were under attack and a vehicle had been blown up. I quickly sorted through it and heard that a HMMWV had been blown up off the road and was thrown into the canal. My heart sunk and waited for the rest of the information. It turned out that the vehicle was in the water, they caught the guy and the US Major that was driving hit a telephone pole. It was sort of like a comic book story. The good guys win in the end. I would get the common question all the time from higher, "Why was a Captain in the turret, or driving the vehicle, or whatever". They never believed me when I told them that was all we had with our teams. Not everyone that worked with us understood that our teams were just 7-10 Soldiers. Eric pulled out everyone from the vehicle through his door and kept everyone from drowning. He is a true hero. He got a little bruised up and he made it out but with a little gash in his leg and his head ringing. He was knocked out but survived. I remember him flying a lot to Balad to get his head checked out. He seemed to attract the enemy and dare them to blow up his vehicle. It happened twice!

One Victory At A Time

We had another important victory for our Iraqis just up the road from us. Remember, we were trying to get them to fight on their own in which they were doing a fine job. Thanks to my boss and the crew, he would lead them all to the water to get them to drink, then think!. We had some really good guys that worked with us. One particular guy I had the utmost respect for. He had seen his day on the battlefield. Ferguson really tried to be happy about what he was doing because I knew deep down inside, he was hating life. He had a really nice smile and could just cheer up your day if you let him. He was that kind of guy. He ran my TOC during the daytime and then some. He had been through enough and unfortunately when you go through those stressful situations, it's time to take a knee. Literally, and catch your breath. He happened to show me a video one day of a Bradley that had got blown up and a guy that flew through the air out of the Bradley. He told me that that guy landed in a small pool of water and survived. The other men in the Bradley unfortunately did not. He started to share with me about how he loved the Army and his men. He really knew a lot about the vehicle and that particular incident. He slowly shared with me that those were his men. I can only tell you that unless you drive a mile in one man's Bradley, you don't know the man. I clearly did not know him. Behind the reluctant smile and the Cuban cigar stood a strong man but who knew firsthand the pain of war and losing a friend. Where ever you are, give me a call.

Trouble At The Local Diner

I really liked going to the Coalition side of the FOB when I had the chance. The food was great and lots of it. The Iraqi army on the other hand did not have these luxuries. For months they had been waiting for their dining facility to open and get food rolling out of it. They would eat in another facility but tension grew between the different Iraqi units when they ate there. And of course there was a lot of accusations and arguments being started about the food and seating with other units. It got so bad one night that some Iraqi guys from a different unit came by and started shooting where our Iraqi guys lived. It was gonna get crazy in this place. (**Inspiration Verse** Psalm 119:79: May those who fear you turn to me, those who understand your statutes."

Revenge

When the BDE S2 (Intelligence Officer) kept asking me to eat with him and his comrades, the polite thing to do was to accept. "Anything less would just be uncivilized". They had no Grey Poupon! So I went with him and again, Saddam's Revenge was waiting for me at the doorstep. I tried to eat and leave as fast as I could. It was a pleasant experience but there was a shortage and I knew these guys were hungry. I knew I was taking from another mouth but I was their guest and they made me eat. When we got back, some of his soldiers came to us showing us stacks of rotten bread.

It had mold on it and it was really gross. Many at the time had been suffering from Taji's Revenge too and they said it was that the food was so bad. I held a straight face and said "No, it couldn't because I just ate it" in a serious non condescending tone. They knew I was full of it but complained anyway. We spoke of how we could fix it when I was done playing. There was nothing I could do until we met with the contractors and they were the ones who could do it. Even our Iraqi boss was upset for his soldiers.

God Willing

I also told them their famous "En Shallah" in which they said I was no good, repeating "Alaniz is no good." I laughed and so did they. (**TIP 8: The idea that God will do for you as He pleases is comforting. As Americans say "God Willing" so do Iraqis which is said "En Shallah."**) All I could do was comfort them and give them assurance they could fix it as soon as the contractors showed up. And rightfully so, cause if you don't feed your troops, they won't fight. If you don't pay them, they won't fight. These same issues we deal with as leaders in the states. You have to remember that they have families too!

Speaking of money, if you ever get a chance to get a lot of money at one time, be sure to get a picture of it. For instance, my wife and I once sold something for a lot of money and had a check that was worth more than I held in a long time. We thought we were so rich but we had to give it to the bank because we owed it and it wasn't really ours. The funny thing is that I wanted to say for a moment I was rich but I was really poor and on welfare working two or three jobs to get through

Ten Thousand Dollars

college. Those were the good o'l days. Anyway, Moudry and Burke and I went for a ride into the neighborhood next door to check on a Mosque and the activity there. I was a little nervous but I had already been on a lot of missions so far but I was finally the convoy commander on this one. Having a lieutenant colonel on every mission I went on kind of kicks the convoy commander thing aside while he takes over. That's just how it goes! As we drove through the neighborhood the locals stopped us and told us of the terrorists that torture and mortar their city. This one local national about 35 years old showed me his back that had bruises all over it. It was horrible.

Another man had his feet beaten with something hard and it had scabs and bruises all over the bottoms of them. He could barely walk. On one of the walls there were hundreds of little holes where a mortar hit. One man had hundreds of the same likeness all over his body where he was standing when a mortar hit. It is difficult for your heart not to go out to these people. This is why we constantly gave as much free stuff and gifts to the people. We wanted them to believe in their future and hope for a tomorrow while not dwelling on the past. We arrived at our destination finding a beautiful Mercedes Benz that ran into a pipe lying on the ground.

Cruising in Style

I think it belonged to these guys we met that were all scrunched into the front seat of a small pick-up. I didn't think it was very strange since I grew up in California where it was common to have all of us packed into the back seat. We should have gone for the Guinness Book of World Records back then. Anyway, one of the other guys on my team noticed it was just a bit odd. It was obvious that he grew up in California too but he was from the Valley. So we pull these Iraqi guys out and they say they gotta go before it gets dark. When we searched them we found a weapon and inside a black bag was literally ten thousand dollars in small bills. If ever I wanted to touch it, that was the time. It felt so good and yet I knew it wasn't ours and they needed to get home. Their story panned out and so they just stayed in custody for a night. Wow, that was crazy!

Right after that when we were leaving, I happened to see an unexploded mortar round or UXO (unexploded ordnance) as we drove by. We could either wait about 4 hours for EOD or just drive by and leave it for the next crew. Well if I didn't call it in, some bad guy would probably use it on one of our vehicles and eventually get me when I came back. So we did the right thing and called the EOD. It wasn't so bad when they got there and we all made it back safely so there was a happy ending that day. **Inspiration Verse** Psalm 119:81 "My soul faints with longing for your salvation, but I have put my hope in your word."

Our Dawg Named Spot

They say that a dog is a man's best friend. That was true for us too, for a while. I know of a story where one particular guy found a dog in Iraq and he wrote a book about it and he end up saving the man's life or something like that. Well I will write a blurb about this dog because she started out cute and cuddly but ended up "twitterpating" with a local dog around the house. Then she began "twitterpating" around in the neighborhood for food, shelter, and a warm bed.

AC Meeting Friends

She later went to seek counseling with the local restaurant owner but found out he was Korean and she quit all ties with him. Her name was AC like Air Conditioning or something. Maybe it was Angie so I got to ask Sterling next time I see him. He's the one who let that nasty thing sleep everywhere in his room. It got so bad that she would just holler in the dark of night and keep me up. I think the Iraqis got fed up with her too!

AC Walking Around

She just got so bad at eating all the trash and rolling in the sewage water, I couldn't stand her. That is all I have to say about AC. May she rest in peace where ever she is. (**TIP 9: Ani Lezemut Chelub translated means "My hand is dirty from the dog." Saying this to someone after you shake hands is probably not the best way to greet someone!**)

A Time For Mourning

August ended a sad month for us as we lost one of our interpreters that had been with the unit prior to us. David was a good man and always helped out. The story goes like this. We had been missing him for a few days as he was supposed to report for work and he didn't. We tried calling and nothing. His wife said he had already left a few days ago because our interpreters called his wife. When the other interpreters told us that he had been captured in Baghdad and tortured for about 7 days before being shot in the head, it was very sad for all of us. I still wonder if he is really dead. Because remember the S4 COL, he may have helped him get into Egypt or Syria when the time was right. If he took his wife I will never know. It is not like we could just drive up to his house and ask his family. It may be one of those Elvis tales and is living life really large. He just may be the missing Elvis of Iraq, but just a poor interpreter. Maybe Hollywood could do a story on this guy. Regardless, somebody got paid for his death. Anyhow, if you are out there David and not gone, send me a letter. Regardless, you will be remembered for always being a giving person. **Inspiration Verse** Psalm 119:82 "My eyes fail, looking for your promise; I say, "When will you comfort me?""

In Conclusion.

So what is Information Operations exactly? I spoke earlier of the Strategic, Operational, and Tactical levels of Information Operations and what those deal with concerning Information. So, Information Operations is the integrated employment of the core capabilities of electronic warfare, computer network operations, psychological operations, military deception, and operations security, in concert with specified supporting and related capabilities, to influence, disrupt, corrupt or usurp adversarial human and automated decision making while protecting our own. Also called IO (Joint Publication 3-13, Feb 2006).

This is why it's so important at the strategic level all the way down to the tactical level. Everyone who is involved is part of the solution to the Information Operations war. Integrating these core capabilities into the units with coordination from the IO officer will assist the commander in understanding and visualizing the informational aspects of the operating environment. This is one of the four core functions of the G/S7 (Overview of Information Operations and Army Information Tasks, Slide 25).

CHAPTER FIVE

I've Fallen and Can't Get Up!

This was truly one of the worst months for me in Iraq. One of the other battalion team members used to talk to me about Soldiers Angels. I said "what the heck is Soldiers Angels?" They are an organization that would send care packages to Soldiers who were deployed. So I began sending them some requests. By Christmas, this organization had sent over 5 Christmas Trees and stockings for all of our team and augmentees. That was around 35 or so guys. They were awesome! Thank you Soldiers Angels. **(TIP 10: If you have Soldiers that have needs, contacting support groups, churches, or Non-Profit organizations to send goodies can bring up morale. Just remember to send a huge Thank You and a picture if available).**

I Need Your Help

Well it wasn't Christmas yet and somebody sent me a care package. I was so happy because it landed on my birthday. I had just finished unloading my vehicle and was heading inside to cool off. My gear was easily over one hundred pounds with SAPPI plates, magazines, Beretta, knee, elbow pads, camelback. It was heavy and my knees hurt too. Just then my back snapped and I couldn't get up. My back hurt so bad I fell straight to the floor. Well I hated that September because I couldn't move for weeks. My boss suggested I move to the division team in Rustamiyah and help out there because I was no good here on the BDE team. I went to the doctor and they said I was fine. The x-rays didn't show the herniated and degenerative disks so they said I was fine. But that is not how I felt. In all the time I was hurt, my boss never came one time to my room and see how I was doing. I won't hold it against him cause I got to learn to let it go. Believe me, it really pissed me off for a long time. But after the Rolling Stone article all the great stuff General McChrystal said, I vowed, and really tried not to say anything really negative about Stan. For one, I don't want some three letter agency guy bothering me or some black suit come harassing me either. It was a rough month but Ernie, Clapp, and others made sure I had food to eat and help me to the latrine. I quickly learned what a piss bottle was. If you collect too many, you can get really sick from inhaling all of that stuff. It was because after drinking liter after liter of water, you got used to peeing all the time. So heading to the nasty pisser was avoidable if possible. I hated September!

I hurt My Back

At the end of September I was doing much better and on the road again. I mean I could feel my legs. When my back did that thing it did, my legs got numb. In Baghdad we snapped this photo as we took a break from driving at Liberty. All those guys are good guys and are greatly missed when they departed with 4th ID. These guys were awesome because they always watched my back.

Our PSD Team

Living by Example

This man started life with no handouts or favors from anyone. I have known him for several years and I have tried to get him to write down what he told me as a young boy. Metcalf grew up during the Vietnam Era and was forced to leave home at a very young age. While in a Prisoner of War camp in the Khmer Rouge hands, he was forced to see and experience what no children or human beings should ever see. Palms were cut so that their leaves were removed from the base of the branch leaving about an inch blade from leaf to leaf. These common manmade saws with teeth could rip the softest flesh and were used to behead others. No touching of the opposite sex was allowed without permission from the elder or leader of the camp said Metcalf. After seeing this horror over and over, Metcalf escaped the camp with his life and nothing else but memories. **Inspiration Verse** Psalm 119:88 "Preserve my life according to your love, and I will obey the statutes of your mouth."

For his troubles in the camp as a boy, scars cover him from the torture he received. After escaping to what I remember him saying a Red Cross camp, they gave him IVs and food for his recovery. He went on to be a successful Non-Commissioned Officer and then later a Commissioned Officer in the US Army. He is a true hero and he is living the American Dream. Because of Virak and his story, it has inspired many who he shares it with about the struggle for life in the most horrific times.

In Conclusion.

Of the Core Functions of Information Operations, Psychological Operations (PSYOP) is probably one of most mis-interpreted realms of the IO spectrum. My earliest introductions to Psychology or what I thought was Psychology were films that dealt with mind power like the Christopher Walken movies or bending spoons with the mind kind of stuff. As a young boy, I thought that they were all related. But what films or examples really deal with Psychology or having influence on others and how they think? Maybe there are Special Forces Teams out there that deal with "The Men Who Stare At Goats" and kill them by mind power, but that is not what this is. There are lots of films for example that deal with psychology but the definition of PSYOP is: To influence the behavior of foreign target audiences (TA) to support US national objectives (FM 3-05.30, Psychological Operations, April 2005). The name recently changed to be not as obvious or threatening. Military Information Support Operations (MISO) is the new name for the "secret squirrel" guys.

CHAPTER SIX

Tourmaline

This month was definitely an eye opener for me. I had been a gunner and TC of a vehicle many times at this point. We had some information and were following up on a lead from an informant that there were some Iraqi officers that had been kidnapped along the Tigris again. It was kind of chilly in the morning because it was about 0200 in the morning as we departed and waited at the house. We were there for a few hours and it was about ten after 0400 when we continued down the road to the next checkpoint so we didn't return the same way. By this time the enemy and he knew exactly when we were on the objective.

I Hear You But Can You Hear Me?

As we continued south I heard a not so loud voice inside me. This is the kind that is different from people saying they have voices in their heads or they see dead people. This was a quiet voice, a soft voice as if warning me of the upcoming trouble. I had been standing up in the turret and was still protected by the shield and glass on the outside of the vehicle. The only thing that could have got me with was with a grenade, RPG, or IED. In that case, you might as well say I was not really protected. I had all of the normal things at my side like extra rounds, water, juice, snacks, NVGs which I had for some time. My eyes were a little tired but I was ok. My weapon had a laser and scope with a light made by Surefire. That is the best light I have ever used. It was almost as good as a headlight on a car but would fit in my hand. Anyway, this voice I knew was not mine cause I liked to stand up so I could see through the glass. Now the voice said "Dan, put your head down". So I immediately put my head down just below the base of the turret where the vehicle met the turret and rested my Night Vision Goggles (NVGs) on the lip. Just then a huge explosion rocked the curbside of my vehicle. I saw an enormous white light and then that is when I put my head down. I lost my vision for a moment but my ears just rang and rang.

The driver of my vehicle was SFC Hale at the time. There were some loud screams that came from the inside of the vehicle and then I heard that we were hit. There was still a lot of chatter from inside the vehicle and I was asking if everyone was ok. I reassured everyone that we weren't hit as I looked over the vehicle as we sped up and pushed through the area. I really couldn't tell for sure about the vehicle but I wanted to calm everyone down. Then the ringing started to sink in more. My ears had this constant ringing which to this day I occasionally have. I should have gone to the aid station but I said what the heck. They rang the entire next day. I think all of us just got used to not relying on the Americans because we didn't live with them. The vehicle behind me had a little damage and that was good enough for me. My vehicle had some dirt and grass on it with some little scratches of tiny rocks that flew at us from the explosion. We never got our package that night but they sure let us know they wanted to give us a night to remember. Hale always watched out for us too and then he also left as his unit pulled out in late October. **(TIP 11: If you hear voices, go see a doctor!)**.

On 09 October we drove back into Saab Al Boor (SAB) to find different routes into the area. The area behind it was being used heavily by anti Iraqi forces to push their fighting into the area as the US Forces from the south made their push Northward. We wanted to make sure the Iraqi Army was using the terrain to their advantage daily and doing patrols in that area. We had found many indications that the area was being used at night for movement and mortar use. As we were leaving by the bridge in SAB, there was a mortar behind us that was really loud. The squadron on the bridge was looking out for us and that is the beauty of counter mortar. The objective is to listen when they fire and attack that same spot with a mortar or an attack. I loved the CAV.

Just Another Note about AC

I think I will talk once more of AC. I snapped some pics of the dog AC this particular day. We had her for some time and I wanted to make sure she stuck in my mind, plus I wanted to send one to the guy that gave us the dog in the first place. That team was back and forth in Rustamiyah and we thought they were going to stay there with the division until things quieted down.

This was the time during the surge which it seemed that every guy with a weapon was using it. Plus, about that time, we got the call that the Division guys captured a guy that was moving or had access to some 155 rounds next to their headquarters. It was about two miles away from our location and we got the word that we were to stay away for a while till it was all cleared up. I think the US higher wanted us to live on the US side but our boss made a good argument about us being in the fight to help them as best as we could. Not a big deal because every day was an adventure. Plus, I don't think they wanted to pour any more money into the area on our behalf. **Inspiration Verse** Psalm 119:90 "Your faithfulness continues through all generations; you established the earth, and it endures."

I Want To Pin Your Rank Like I Got Mine

I was at the division headquarters everyday anyway so I knew what was going on with the situation. I had to make a meeting every day or so and speak with the Major up there on the progress of missions and the way ahead for the Iraqi Tank BDE. This is where I first met English. They were of significance because there were only Ten Divisions at the time of Iraqi Army and only one of those was a Tank Division. The first brigade was down in Baghdad and we were standing up the second one. It was about this time or so that our Iraqi boss came back from Baghdad wearing General rank. I was a little shocked because in our Army we make a big hoopla about that kind of stuff. It's in the paper, in Army Times, and everyone knows. He just went to Baghdad and then came back a General. Wish that was true for us. Just somebody wave their hand up there at DA and I will change my rank ASAP. No questions asked. When I got pinned, my shoulder hurt from the pins going into my skin. Let me show you COL how it really done, US style! Anyways,

I continued to eat breakfast with those guys up there at Division almost every day since we arrived in country and it was good.

I usually got up in the morning and took a shower if I felt like walking into the shower dungeon. By this time I was used to not taking showers daily but my clothes missed some washing. After missing some washings, my clothes would stand up on their own. Plus, most of the time I was just so tired to get them to the US FOB and it took some time to do that. Anyway, I would make it up there to division headquarters and these guys would have already gone to the US side to get boxed breakfast so we would eat. The breakfast was your normal eggs, cereal, sausage, pancakes or French toast. I would sit down with CPT Shawn English cause he was the night battle captain and we would chat about stuff. Really nice guy and was always tense with energy. I think he hated being inside everyday but somebody has got to do it. They did an excellent job at making the TOC a really good one for the Iraqi Army. When I would bring the Iraqi training updates of all that the Iraqi soldiers were doing, I would have to hang around a bit longer. All the lessons learned for them would help them win the war against the anti Iraqi forces. We ate and had this routine until they moved to Rustamiyah sometime later. **Inspiration Verse** Psalm 119:92 "If your law had not been my delight, I would have perished in my affliction."

Scott's Coming To Town

I was really lonely during these times cause all I did was work, eat and sleep. It never seemed like there was a break for me. Poor me, I know but it was a crazy job. I was going crazy and needed a break. We kept talking about R&R but our boss made it clear we weren't going on Rest and Relaxation. He wanted his team all the time, everyday ready and available to fight the good fight. So in saying all of that, we never got R&R.

So I had a friend come to visit me on official business. Scott and I met in 2001 when going through Officer Candidate School at Fort Benning. He is one of the smartest, roughest, loudest guys that I ever met next to my brother-in-law Scott. When he said he was from Jersey, I admit I never met anyone from Jersey. The guy's from Jersey got a lot of pride and talk tough but Scott always backed it up. I used to go over

The General, me and Scott

to his apartment when he lived in El Paso and hang out with him. He was an Air Defense Officer and had been in Iraq before me a few years earlier. Now he was an Aide De Camp of sorts and I asked if he could get on a bird and come and see us while his boss was visiting the US side of the base. He did come to see me and that was one of the most memorable times I had with him. He only had a little time of about an hour and it went fast. I snapped this picture of him when I showed him the cache of weapons and RPGs we had lying around the boss's office.

Scott in His Movie Premier

Our boss liked to restore some of the weapons we captured and he had a huge arsenal. He had a real love for history and liked to work with his hands. So they came and went and that was the best part of October. Who flies through all kinds of rough terrain and all kinds of danger to see a buddy? I will tell you he is the only one that did. **Inspiration Verse** Psalm 119:93 "I will never forget your precepts, for by them you have preserved my life."

Waking Of The Lambs

We made one more search in the early morning on several houses that we had intel that were bad guys and was directly across from a Mosque. There was a tendency to have some small arms fire and then run into a Mosque. Obviously we couldn't enter the Mosque so they would get away. The rule was to surround the Mosque and let other Iraqis enter the mosque. If you entered, that would be very very bad. We caught on but it was still a headache. This particular mission was a dead end but SFC Clapp said I had let the lambs out of their stable. He was joking but the boss had his infamous frown on his face. If I did let them out, it wasn't on purpose of course. Can you think of any other reasons that they hated us over there? I was just trying to search the area. If your gonna hide stuff, who would look under a pile of crap? (**TIP 12: Never, Never, Never enter a Mosque. This will get you into serious trouble with the Iraqis and US**).

October came and went. I know Ramadan was one of the reasons the intensity picked up quite a bit. Who wants to fight in the cold? Not yet, it wasn't cold yet especially where we were at. We were making sure that the roads were clear on the main route from Baghdad to Balad for all of the people that were on Hajj to go north. People would travel great distances to do this one act of their life and wanted to get there in one piece. It would really stink to wait all your life to do this sacred act and then get shot on the way there. That is a tragedy if I will say. The people would travel on the road and park and camp on the sides and rest there until they got moving again. When the curfew hit at 9 pm, everyone had to be off of the road. And I mean everybody. If not, they either could get kidnapped or taken to prison for the night. Nothing good ever happens at night a leader once told me while living in a bad neighborhood. He was right no matter what bad neighborhood you live in. Night is the worst. (**TIP 13: Ramadan is a very serious time for Muslims in which they do a lot of praying and fasting. Try not to eat food or drink in front of them. Most are fasting and it may be very tempting for them so respect their culture and beliefs with the utmost respect.**)

Goodbye Team

October was also the time when we had to say goodbye to all of the Infantry guys as their US Division was leaving after a long 15 months. I wasn't happy at all because seeing all those guys leave was heartbreaking. It was also very exciting for them as well because they were short. When people are short, or have just days to leave, they start talking about all the good stuff from home and the things they are going to do when they get back to Hood. For some, they would be coming back for a second or third tour. For others they just had enough and wanted to get out. Who could blame them because the Army is not for everyone and after that year, some just wanted to go to college and move on. I miss them all.

In Conclusion.

Many of the best military leaders in the past used military deception as a means to attempt to win their battles against sometimes superior or outnumbering forces on the sea or land. During the Gulf War the use of military deception was used by our military leaders to deceive Saddam's forces, and it worked. Iraq believed there would be a large naval force landing with thousands of Marines to engage on the beaches from the north and south. General Schwartskoff used this to his advantage and set his military to outflank the Iraqis and win in the initial conflict. Military Deception comprises actions executed to deliberately mislead adversary military decision makers as to friendly military capabilities, intentions, and operations, thereby causing the adversary to take specific actions (or inactions) that will contribute to the accomplishment of the friendly mission (FM 3-13, 2003).

CHAPTER SEVEN

Sour November

I was so happy to see November this year. I knew in just a few days I would be heading off for my two weeks leave to see my family. Josh's birthday had already past in June, Matthews birthday was in August, and September was Mindy's and mine. November happened to be my in-laws birthdays as well so I just wanted to get home in once piece. I tried to give as much as I could to our day and night battle captains to do the missions and take over the meetings for me while I was gone. It went over smoothly. These guys were professionals and I had no choice to leave them with what I had to do there in Taji. Some of the other guys on my team didn't think so but oh well.

I'm On My Way Home

When I got on the helicopter from Taji to Baghdad that night, I could feel the strain just fall off my shoulders. I also had this uncontrollable grin that I couldn't remove if you had a chisel. I had been carrying so much weight from that time there in Taji that all I could do was smile. I was sleeping in a clean cot the next night until my plane left for Kuwait and I knew it. When I got to Kuwait I waited another day or so before I got on the plane to Dallas. I had clean fresh water in Kuwait to take a really long shower and I didn't care this time. It was as if the dirt just came right off as compared to Taji. InTaji, the water made me deformed because it wasn't treated as good as living on the US FOB. I still had to explain the sixth toe that grew mysteriously when I got home. At this point, I just wanted to thank God for that entire time. He had done for me and protected me from all the dangers. He was faithful to the end. **(TIP 14: When drinking water that is not treated, be sure that CIPRO is available).** It was better than living on a ship. You would end up smelling like JP5 after a shower. Wait a second, yes I would smell worse after getting out of the shower? Down in the bottom of the ship, the fuel would sometimes get into the water and then be used for showers. It was an unavoidable travesty and paradox to have gas water and not salt water for showers while in the middle of the ocean.

When I got to Dallas, we were greeted by volunteers from the community that gave us a care bag and some snacks. That is never done anywhere else in the world as good as Texas. Texas is an awesome state because I have been here for some years now. If we could fix the local tax I would be happier. When I arrived at the airport to meet my family it was a great reunion. I hugged my boys who came running to me and it was a great day. My youngest son Andrew just gave me that look again like "What chu talking about Willis." He would end up warming up to me during my stay. It went so fast. All I wanted was to eat of the different foods in the neighborhood. I had thin crust pizza that just melted in my mouth. It was the kind that had four different types on one pizza on the same pan. Although they were all good I loved the one that had sun dried tomatoes with fresh mozzarella and basil. I have to say that the pizza at the Oar House in Portsmouth New Hampshire where I now live, is also an incredible pizza. Good stuff. I had McDonald's, Taco Bell, and lots of bread. **Inspiration Verse** Psalm 119:95 "The wicked are waiting to destroy me, but I will ponder your statutes."

Bread Made to Order

My wife knows I love bread just as much as her dad. Joe is a fine man and very smart. He once laid a fresh loaf of bread next to me when I awoke at his house on a vacation. We flew all day and I was smoked when we arrived that night. When I woke up the next morning and saw it, it was one of the nicest things they ever done for me and they have done a lot I might add. Joe works hard and doesn't know when to stop sometimes. He runs circles around me when I visit. He is always cooking too just like his son Scott. Scott's restaurant in New Hampshire called The Dolphin Striker where I now manage, and is one of the finest around and people drive from all over to visit. He once showed me how he makes his Italian meatballs. He used three different meats including veal, hamburg, and pork in equal parts and mixed them together with herbs and spices. You can use other meats but this time this is what he used. Once we put them into bite size balls then we cooked them halfway in Olive oil. That was what their grandmother did when she made hers. We finished them off in by letting them sit in the gravy. Well "gravy" means sauce in the Boston area. Their sauce is another story. If you wanted the big meatballs they were great too. If Bobby Flay ever challenged him it might be close!

Sharing food with family is an important thing that I grew up with. Being from Ventura California, my family had many gatherings. Most centered around food and fun. I tried to show that same hospitality to the Iraqis that I lived with so they could see that I was for real and sharing was part of our Mexican and Indian culture as well. They began to see that I was friendly and giving just like many of their people. I tried on many occasions to give some of the treats to them so they could taste what we ate in the states. Gum, chocolate, sugar treats, drinks, Gatorade, food, and anything I could get my hands on, we would eat together. **Inspiration Verse** Psalm 119:96 "To all perfection I see a limit; but your commands are boundless."

Hanging in the Work Lounge

They did the same for me as well. In a small room upstairs in the large hallway, there was a room just big enough for a plastic table and several to sit and watch the TV on plastic lawn chairs. The daily plates of food that came from the Iraqi chow hall were stacked up for those who were on duty to eat when they had the chance. The bread that they ate was very much like a tortilla so I naturally packed it up with whatever was available and chomped down. My counterpart took great pleasure as I ate and shared his customs with me and I with him. This would continue many times throughout the year.

I consider the awakening that I saw in relation to the food aspect of their culture to be a very important part of living. I have never been to someone's house that I didn't want to try some of their home made cooking. This is the same with their culture. Food has always been the focus or the appetizer to business and relationships. Dignitaries and businessman and women understand that eating dinner and getting to know someone is so important before talking business. When I grew up, the older women and wives would cook and serve the men in one room. When the men were done, the women would all eat together. It could have been because the women or in my case aunts, just didn't want to sit with their husbands and my uncles. Regardless, the men served the men and cleaned up after them. It was obviously this way because women were at their homes and men had to do this. I think they loved it too.

I think we lost this in the United States during my growing up years in the 70s with the TV Trays and TV dinners. It was fun as a kid to have the different kinds of foods separated and cake or pie on the plate for dessert but I think it really took a lot away from our culture. I think it is important for families to sit down and look into each others eyes at least once a day. Not that TV dinners are bad but without eating with someone leads to a separated lifestyle with family. Our lives become so busy that we cannot slow down or don't have time for one another. We have to get back to the basics and make cookies together, set the table nightly and do the dishes together. We need this in our culture in order to survive as a people that can be intimate with each other without feeling as though it is only on holidays we do these things. In the movie "The Blind Side", Sandra Bullocks' character realized this and moved the family from the living room where they were watching TV into the dining room where they all ate together.

Its not that it should be done everyday but when we look at each other across the table and ask how our day was and what was important about it, that is how we keep from growing apart. It is a way to teach our children about relationships and that it takes effort to keep the things we love.

Many times when we sat down at the table in Iraq with our counterparts, it was the way we shared and ate together that brought us together. Sitting down for tea for an hour after a meal was so relaxing and comforting that it shows that there are many things in life besides the war that was going on that beg for our time. There is a book called "Three Cups of Tea" which deals with that relationship building and the necessity to share ones culture prior to talking business in Afghanistan. Being a Hispanic, I don't want to generalize and I am being funny but I should write a book called, "Three Shots of Tequila". If you want to get to know someone from across the table, you got to eat and drink and share their culture with them. That is how you make lasting relationships. What about when the fast food business will begin to erupt in the Middle East? How has it affected their culture? Will those that are older begin to hate and resent what westerners brought to them or can it be used for good? The capitalistic dream is alive over there and they want to have their dreams come true economically as well as us that are in the US.

I believe that the fast food industry will have a direct impact on their culture and for them to figure out the balance of keeping century old traditions alive in their part of the world. This will be a challenge for the generations to come. Commercialism will impact their way of thinking and the struggle to hold onto their identity as a people will also be a challenge. This is the same thing that the Jewish people have fought for centuries.

In Conclusion.

The digital technological age is here. We can't run from it but others must learn to embrace it as well. Computer Network Operations comprise computer network attack; computer network defense; and related computer network exploitation enabling operations (FM 3-13, NOV 2003). Does the Information Operations Officer fix computers or write programs? Many confuse this with what the Signal Officer (S6) does and manage to not fully understand how the IO integrates this capability as the spokesperson into the operation. Again, it takes the coordination of the entire staff to use these capabilities.

CHAPTER EIGHT

Christmas Jingles

After sleeping in and eating as much as possible on my visit home, it was time to go back to Taji. When I arrived in Baghdad, I couldn't get a flight back so I had to wait another day because it was so busy. I arrived back to the White House and got the word that we had lost a division guy. CPT English was a good man and I missed having breakfasts with him and sharing about our time there in Iraq. It hit our division guys really hard too. There were eleven of them that trained with us at Fort Hood and they were all fun to be with when we weren't doing busy stuff.

While at North Fort Hood, we ended our training at a restaurant in Killeen. But we all lied around on our backs when we could or when there was no training. I set up Ernie because he and Ross were always playing jokes on everybody else so, since I knew him a little more and knew his panties wouldn't get all in bunch, I let him nap with his little friends.

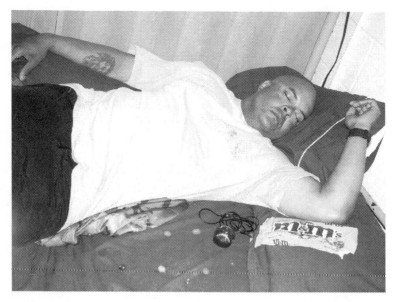

Ernie and M&M Friends!

Building A Dysfunctional Team

That is when we got to see all of the teams not wearing green for the first time. It is awkward when you see people not wearing the uniforms who always wear it day in and day out. On top of calling everyone by their last name, hearing their first name was just as awkward too.

Team 0920 PIC

Each had on his own style of clothes and you could tell who liked motorcycles, who wore the khakis and was straight forward as if coming from church and the guys that had the baggy ones. It brought back memories of when going on pass for the first time and not having regular civilian clothes straight out of basic training. In the winter you knew who was in the service because they had sneakers or running shoes that were all beat up, blue jeans and a brown or white t-shirt. The black belt had a smooth finish along with the black trench coat. The clean hair cut didn't help much either. What a dork I was! Everyone who has been in the service knows what I am talking about. Just go hang outside of a basic training post and you will see. **Inspiration Verse** Psalm 119:98 Your commands make me wiser than my enemies, for they are ever with me."

Can't You Just Rest for One Day?

When I was gone on Leave, I got the word that my boss's vehicle was hit by and EFP (Explosive formed Projectile) which went through his door and rear of the curb side of the HMMWV. I thought that would be the kind of thing that would slow someone down but not my boss. When I saw the damage on the armor, I was really taken back and thought someone could have been seriously hurt. My boss is invincible. I have heard stories of guys that lived to be a hundred years old that smoked like chimneys and drunk like fish. I now believe it is because God is giving us many chances to see that He is not a bad guy like many make Him to be.

Soldiers Angels to the Rescue

By this time Soldiers Angels had sent me many boxes of goodies. I had never seen gummy Eye balls, or Gummy Teeth. I had dozens of boxes in which I put as much stuff from the packages as I could into each stalking. I even went to the PX there on Taji to find the additional ten or so missing Christmas stalkings so everyone could have one. I put names on them for every Soldier so that he could experience Christmas like home. We decorated the Christmas tree in the main room as to not offend the Iraqis and put all of the stalkings under the tree. When some Iraqis had seen that I had a tree in my room they wanted one too! So I took one down to the General and gave it as a gift. He had his jundee (soldiers) put it the hallway. I don't think their religious leaders would have approved of the Christmas tree but Santa Claus didn't mind. This is a tremendous victory for sharing our culture with ones who did not see Christmas as His Story.

Christmas With Iraqi's

They knew the importance of Christ and the Judeo Christian beliefs so they were very proud to show it off. It's not every day you have a Muslim have a Christmas tree in their hallway. Maybe that was a first? Soldiers Angels even sent us a CD player in which we used on the top patio. I got to admit that without Soldiers Angels coming to the rescue and all of the packages, that wouldn't have been Christmas. We even had extra snacks for our Iraqi counterparts who were very surprised at the individual candies and rappers. It was like giving candy to a child for the first time. In the movie "Band of Brothers" when the little boy ate the Hershey's chocolate bar, it was like that moment, just priceless!

A guy who I recently met said in Vietnam, the children acted the same way when US Soldiers gave them the little peanut butter candies.

Some of the kids there in Vietnam would also give little gifts back that were made of metal and had short fuses (grenades). I guess every war is similar in story besides the death. **Inspiration Verse** Psalm 119:103 "How sweet are your words to my taste, sweeter than honey to my mouth."

Christmas should always be a special time no matter where you are or what your religion. Everyone knows it is the season of giving. Well I had had my Christmas's away from home just like the next guy. The first year in the military, I also remember eating cold turkey and taters for that first Thanksgiving away from home cause I was sick in the barracks. I couldn't' make it to the dining facility so another recruit brought me my dinner. I can't remember clearly but it was definitely one and maybe two in the next few years that I missed being with family. It's a very lonely for the service member. Since 9/11 I think I spent two more away from home but just barely missing other holidays. I know I missed countless birthdays and anniversaries of 12 years being married. (**TIP 15: If possible, try not to talk religion. After developing a comfortable friendship and open conversation, that is probably a good time.**)

Time To Make The Fire

This time was going to be different. When Soldiers Angels sent us boxes of Marshmallows I didn't know how to separate them for the rest of the other guys. Maybe Kraft could package them individually and make Smores out of them for the children taking box lunches? By this time we had made a nice pit on the roof where we would bar-b-que or roast stuff. Even our interpreters would join in and make us good food that they brought from the economy. Nothing in this world is more important than eating with your family or brothers and comrades. This was no exception. I invited my counterparts consisting of COLs and below to join us. The General was busy or something but I am not sure. So they came up to our area, walked through our hooches and stood around the fire pit for the first time since we had been there. We had bags of the really Big Marshmallows made by Kraft. They will stay good for a long time since they are packaged well and keep the air inside. Zien means "good" and Kula means "very" and so you have "Very Good."

I got a marshmallow and stuck it in the fire and made it so it was consumed by the fire. The flame surrounded the entire marshmallow and got nice and crispy just the way I like it. It was gooey hot. When I blew out the flame and jammed it in my mouth, they were all taken back. They had never seen anything like that. As a matter of fact, they never saw a marshmallow. The Iraqi COL asked me "shinuwa marrsh-mellow?" What is this thing that you do? How you eat such hot thing or "Harran" thing they would ask? They couldn't get past the fact that although it was so hot, how could it cool down and not burn my mouth. They were afraid and hesitant to do what I was doing. I told them to eat the stupid thing. After about 20 marshmallows and ten minutes later, the young Iraqi captain finally did it. It was the best part of the night. Then they all got it as he convinced the others to eat it. They devoured the bag and wanted some to take to the others who were on duty. I opened another bag and gave some out to them so they could give to others to try. We stood around the warm fire and continued to eat the marshmallows and share stories with one another.

Sharing Customs

I told them they were the first Iraqis to eat marshmallows because they had never heard of them. Saddam has everything and we had nothing. They would say we had no Coke or TV or anything. "This is the first for us" they would say. When they all agreed that this was the first time of really sharing this incredible experience, all I could do was listen intently to their stories. Inside of me, my heart leaped with joy. It was so funny to see my interpreters to act like it was a common, normal experience, this thing of eating marshmallows and show the others for the first time to roast marshmallows, was if they had done this their entire lives. But minutes earlier, they were asking the same funny questions. "How do you eat it if it is on fire?" "Won't it burn you Alaniz?" In their culture, it is very good if you know something that the other don't, this include customs or just basic knowledge. It gives the impression that you are wise! Our interpreters thought they were so awesome and they were. They acted just like little kids. (**TIP 16: If you know that an Iraqi does not know the answer, do not press him in front of others. This is a sign of weakness and ignorance. Remember,** they believe that Allah has put their leaders there in those positions and loyalty is very important to them, or at least the appearance of loyalty).

Interpreters

I had shared with them that in the US, this was a custom that we did when sitting around a fire or Ranger TV. This was done with family or friends at all times of the year. They had done something no other Iraqis had done before and it meant something to me and them. They knew that in their culture they were changing too and this was a sign of the times.

From Good Americans Pockets, That's How

This was such a historic moment for me and the realization that their culture was to changing. The Iraqi people are developing their culture as we did some 200 years ago. It is exciting to see the great changes that many of the reporters do not share on US Television. Seeing the hospitals, schools, roads, lights, electricity and many other things being built by their own hands with US support is tremendously inspiring when it is they who are thanking for the help. Many times it was not the government who did these things, but good Americans that gave out of their own pockets like Hurricane Katrina but that information never gets reported either. Seeing children with new schoolbooks that have No Saddam propaganda is a huge victory. Watching a singing show like Iraqi Idol for the first time was also an experience. **Inspiration Verse** Psalm 119:105 "Your word is a lamp to my feet and a light for my path."

When roasting marshmallows is done with the Iraqi people, it is very much like the shedding of things of the past. Watching the outer side of the marshmallow burn and become dead while waiting inside is a warm, gooey, sweet treat waiting to be eaten. Iraqi people are waiting to eat the very best of life from the many natural resources from the land, and the building of a confident, proud army, and culture. Remember that their land is the oldest of all time and their culture has rich heritage. They are in many ways rebuilding new lives and it is as exciting like roasting marshmallows in front of a glowing campfire.

I wasn't always a prankster. But many times I was playing tricks on them and giving them hell when I could. It was in good humor and they would do it back to me. When I was invited to lunch with the General and his battalion commanders almost every day, they would have some foods that would take me a minute to get used to but then they would warm on me.

One of my favorite adventurers is Anthony Bourdaine. He would have had no problem eating many of the great tastes as well. There were parts of the fish or things I didn't recognize that were just too much for me to stomach but I ate it and was soon a convert of Iraqi cuisine. If you had menudo before, you should be all right but not everyone could do this. My wife gets nauseous when she smells it. So the General would take from his plate in his hand and put it to my lips. I knew it would be very disrespectful if I didn't so I had to eat it. "Lord, please bless this food for my body and stomach as I eat." This was my constant prayer as they sprung it on me. But I couldn't refuse because they knew it was an insult. They would laugh out loud as they saw our expressions. It was kind of funny if you think of it. Kind of like a college trick or something.

(TIP 17: If a man wants to hold your hand, do not resist and pull your hand away. This is a deep sign of respect and genuine liking of the purest form from one man to another. It is looked upon with favor).

I Never Went Over The Edge With My Pranks

One day I got my counterpart S3 back and the other guys on shift. I am not Jewish but love the people very much because Arabs and Israelis are cousins. I have this Jewish Star of David on my Dog tags that I got as a memento twenty years prior and I would pull out and show them. My counterpart knew I was joking and saw the humor while I would wait for the reaction of the others Iraqis. My counterpart would let them in on the joke later. He was good like that. If the nuns in catholic school knew I would turn out like this, they would have said more prayers for me back then. **Inspiration Verse** Psalm 119:107 "I have suffered much; preserve my life, O LORD, according to your word."

In Conclusion.

There are still several other Core Capabilities of Information Operations which I haven't touched on. My use of electronics is very limited as I remember trying to build a electric clock or something in electric shop while in high school. Believe it or not, this is just one element of the electromagnetic spectrum. Many enemies have used this capability and very old tactics to try to defeat superior technological armies and have succeeded. The point is to be the best at what you do and this will be a challenge to every active military army throughout the world. Electronic warfare is any military action involving the use of electromagnetic and directed energy to control the electromagnetic spectrum or to attack the enemy (FM 3-13, NOV 2003).

CHAPTER NINE

January is Freezing

The weeks leading up to 7 January 07 had a lot of planning to do because this was going to be the biggest Iraqi Joint mission for 2007. At this time the surge in Baghdad was going well with the pressure being put on by all sides. The Prime Minister Mr. Maleki had just made our tank brigade his Ready Reserve which meant they were to be ready at any times notice to go and fight in Baghdad or wherever he needed our Iraqi Brigade to go. We had prepared the Soldiers to conduct Cordon and Searches in which our Iraqi Brigade Headquarters (Scouts) would do a lot of the training. Ernie had overseen this with many of our team like Clapp and Hale.

The day would include Iraqi Special Police, Iraqi Special Forces, Iraqi (Mechanized) BMPs from one of our Battalions, and T-72 Tanks from our Brigade, along with the Generals TOC. It was a huge procedure just to get all the vehicles in unison to where they were to operate. The integration of all those there had with literally hundreds of vehicles which was a great success to see the Iraqis working together despite all their competition against one another. The Iraqi Army would say the police were crooked, and the Iraqi police would say that the Army was lazy and weak. This went back and forth and so on and so on. A lot of coordination was done through the MiTTs and SPiTs (Special Police Teams) who brought those Iraqi leaders to our Iraqi boss's TOC and private study for coordination. My boss was well up to it and very charismatic and it just seemed like it was nothing for him to brief this kind of stuff. He always showed himself to be very capable. Half of his years in the service were literally spent out of the US. That would explain the easiness of the job. He could do it blindfolded. Did I forget to mention it was also very cold.

Me in Baghdad

I was also confident in our Iraqi Scouts because they were the lead on many of the missions done by our Iraqi Brigade and requested by our sister unit in the CAV. At first it was to put more than an Iraqi face on it and we were at the point of them taking the lead on almost all of the missions but it evolved more than just that. They were getting that confident. Chief Warrant Officer Ali, the OIC is cleaning his vehicle on the 6th getting ready for his mission. He was a happy quite man before he left this earth. He gave his life the next day for his country.

Kids, Just Stay In The Vehicle!

I gave the convoy brief that morning on the 7th early in the morning. It was really early in the morning and nobody in Taji was up to include the dogs. The entire road on the Iraqi side was filled with vehicle after vehicle waiting to leave the base. I told the drivers to stay in their seats and wait and be ready as I gave them the safety brief. I told the gunners to stay in their seats and sit below the glass shields for protection against snipers. There was a habit to forget these things and go Rambo or do whatever you felt like. Iraqi drivers would sometimes get out of their vehicles and get a smoke while there was a lag in the battle. This day would prove to be no different. **Inspiration Verse** Psalm 119:109 "Though I constantly take my life in my hands, I will not forget your law."

As the early morning cold moved out and the heat of the day could be felt through my armor, there was a real peace that I had about this

In Baghdad on M1113

mission. We set up our TOC for our Iraqi boss as he gave orders to the men from a distance. I snapped this photo of the M1113 that the Iraqi's had. I would hate to ride in this. It was so thin you could see my shadow from the outside. It had very thin walls and armor on this vehicle. Definitely not for me!

After my Iraqi boss had situational awareness we decided to check on the area that was being cleared. The radio cracked wide open again and said that CPT Lane had been hit in the chest by a sniper. There was lots of gunshots from a M240 about a mile away. It stopped and then there was some small arms fire. A HMMWV raced by us just to our North in order to get to Taji for medical help. I quickly used my radio and called it in to the Taji FOB that we had a Soldier WIA en route. We were all worried for Lane and I said a little prayer for him as his vehicle sped by. We moved to the assembly area and got out of the vehicles to give escort for our boss and Iraqi boss. Some of the Iraqi men had found a small cache with fuses and mortars. This was a good find and proved to be good to get these weapons out of the hands of the enemy. I went with two other officers and we cleared a small area. I found a pile of washer timers that were in a little trash area. The timers were used for IEDs and I snagged a picture and picked them up for evidence to be used at a later date.

Smile, Let's Take A Picture

The Soldier from COMCAM (Combat Camera) was right next to us snapping all kinds of photos on the battlefield. Another civilian was hit in the leg and our Iraqi medics treated his would. Funny thing about an AK 47 is that it leaves a good nickel size wound at the entrance. The exit is much different. We got the word that Lane was ok and that the round hit him in the chest and the body armor crystallized around the round to keep it from penetrating the entire armor. Those plates are awesome. Iraqi soldiers had metal plates that were just as good but they were heavy. Lane was confined to quarters for rest because his chest was black and blue. He was just happy to be alive. (**TIP 18: When searching groups where women are present, make sure a male Soldier does not go near a female. Let this searching be done by other Iraqi Women Soldiers or US Females.**)

When I got back to the main area where we had parked our vehicles, this was one time that I couldn't hold back. We had some guys of higher rank than me that wanted to come and support us for this mission and were sitting in the back seat of one of the HMMWVs. We had already parked for some time and I couldn't figure out why they were still in the vehicle just like "Driving Miss Daisy." I literally lost my temper and had a few words with this senior officer as I yelled at him and his buddy to get out and pull security. This was one of the first times I yelled at a LTC. The reason they didn't get out is because all of the Iraqi soldiers around us were still on a knee or in the prone because this sniper had not been caught yet. They were just simply afraid. I let them have it! They got out of the vehicle as I opened the door and told them to pull security. They heard what happened to the guy with the hole in his leg and didn't want that to happen to them. **Inspiration Verse** Psalm 119:111 "Your statutes are my heritage forever; they are the joy of my heart."

The Iraqi National Flower

The time spent out in the area was just about over in the early afternoon in the area west of Taji and we were going to secure the route out of the area with several HMMWVs. We took three HMMWVs and set up just behind the local market. All of a sudden a round shot out of the air and Ali was hit. I had never seen an Iraqi Death Blossom before that time but many told me about it. There were about 5 Iraqi soldiers in front of my vehicle shooting in a 360 degree pattern. They were right in front of my vehicle and it was crazy. They didn't know who they or what they were shooting at but they were going to expend all of their ammunition. This had been done several times in the past and then they would get overrun because they had no ammo left. I tried to get out of my vehicle and check on Ali as Clapp said over the radio a guy was hit. I called it in to the TOC and again tried to get out of my vehicle to secure the area. **(TIP 19: Never get in the way of the Death Blossom!)**

I told the other vehicles to secure the road and sides so we could cordon the area. DOC was already over Ali trying to clear his throat so he could get oxygen into his lungs. I saw the round hole just over his temple. I was broken and so were his men because we knew we lost a good man that day. We told the Iraqi TOC to tell the chain of command and within minutes, BMPs, Tanks, HMMWVs were all over the area. I called in the cavalry and the grid and they were over us looking for egress routes. An Abrams showed up as well and many US HMMWVs and then I saw the 1-1 BDE CDR, COL Funk walking toward me. I gave him the sitrep and then moved on. Our Iraqi boss was really upset because he was good friends with Ali. They were like family. That entire area was searched within a half an hour as the Iraqi soldiers started shooting at anything that moved. People in the village were running for cover. I tried to stop and calm down the troops but they were enraged.

The Cross Dresser

The Iraqis said that the sniper would dress like a woman while his comrade placed the weapon and he took the shot. When it was over, he would leave dressed as a female and the spotter would take the weapon. It made sense because we could not catch them. Maybe this guy liked to dress up like women, who knows? I think you would have to really play the part of the girl and get good at it if you wanted to do it successfully. **Inspiration Verse** Psalm 119:114 "You are my refuge and my shield; I have put my hope in your word."

Just a few months ago when we lost our friends, our Soldiers, and comrades, they too were very sad at our loss and understood why some of our team members were acting hostile. When their Soldier was hit, it was just like a complete reversal of what we experienced and just as painful for me. I went to the area where Ali had stayed and looked and spoke with many of his team before the wake. They were all broken up. Imagine many guys in a single room with just barely enough to keep them warm, not the cleanest of areas, and second hand bunks and mattresses. Not only did they serve their country but they usually had little to do it with. My heart went out to them every time I went to their hooches. At the wake many gathered in a large room where the center of the large room was open and a jundee served chai, and passed out cigarettes. The leaders sat around and talked and prayed and had light conversation over his wake.

Losing a Comrade

The 1-1 BDE CDR and some of his leadership were there which showed their concern and utmost respect for the Iraqi Army and their loss. It wasn't the first time he came and it wouldn't be the last either.

After about a half an hour, the tables were set in the hallway. It was about a thirty yards long and tables filled the center. The tables were set with many of the favorite dishes including wonderful rice with raisins, and dates. It was light and very tasty. The chicken and lamb was extremely good with fresh bread. I ate until I couldn't eat anymore. This was one of the many funerals that I had experienced while in Iraq to include US Servicemen. **(TIP 20: Make every effort to be present at funerals. Their friendship is deeper than blood).**

Of the many men that we went to lay to rest, the most heart wrenching moment is when the individual's names are called out loud. The role call done by the first sergeant yells out the names of the individuals that are gone and calls their name several times. After the playing of Taps, I cannot help to hold back the tears of the men lost. I cry inside of my heart and feel the depression of losing that person forever. We remember just sitting with that person, eating a meal or laughing out loud and then it's all gone.

When I see the bands play and musicians walk singing "When the Saints Come Marching In," Iraqi customs were very similar to what we do in the states. People gathered and then celebrated his life. It was very profound and reminiscent of things done in the South and New Orleans. When Ali died, some of his soldiers had enough and called it quits for the army. It happened occasionally when a soldier would just get up from his post, pick up his helmet and weapon and turn them into the officer in charge. If they were at a checkpoint they would just get into their civilian clothes and then jump in a cab. They would be gone and never return. Some would take weapons and then the Iraqis would have to go and find them to get their stuff back. **Inspiration Verse** Psalm 119:116 "Sustain me according to your promise, and I will live; do not let my hopes be dashed."

The system of the Iraqi Army still did business like the past. They marched the same and did a lot of movements in battle the same way they always did. Their influence came from the British and I would do competitions with the other Iraqis and see who could do the best marching. The best part was the upside down hand salute which would get lots of laughs from everyone as they said I didn't do it right. It reminded me of Benny Hill. They thought they were better but I couldn't tell the difference. It was a pride thing. When I did drill and ceremony according to the Army, they thought it was boring and not flashy. I just didn't know how to do all the fancy stuff. Who could blame if we never had anyone who could represent drill in a awesome way. If I knew how to spin an M4 like the Marines, I could have made my money. Maybe next time. Competing seemed to be fun and we did it every now and then.

At the middle of the month the Iraqi boss hosted a feast in which the 1-1 CAV BDE CDR, the Iraqi FOB US supervisor, and BN and BDE MiTTs came to eat at his location. For the first time, I saw everyone together eating and enjoying the food. It was another delicious meal by our hosts. We ate with the General and this was definitely a treat for us all. Of course, most of my team did not show due to the food but again, I loved it.

Eucalyptus grows here too?

January was brutally cold for me. Growing up in southern CAL, I never like the cold. I happened to snatch a picture of a guy who was Jay Leno's twin there on the street. We all knew it was Jays long lost brother. If I show it he may lose his life so I kept it out of the book. When the temperature is on average seventy three degrees year round, you kind of get spoiled from it all. The beautiful avocado trees and orchards that split the Ojai valley through Montecito was breathtaking. In many ways the strong wind of eucalyptus trees seemed to remind me of Ventura daily. **Inspiration Verse** Psalm 119:117 "Uphold me, and I will be delivered; I will always have regard for your decrees."

When we visited the DIV team there in Baghdad, it was a good but short visit. They worked long and hard too. Their outside walls of the compound were smaller than the building they lived in, making excellent targets for those around outside the area.

Anyone Want An Egg?

They were getting barriers and anything they could get their hands on to build it up. A single strand of concertina wire was around their TOC and I know they didn't feel safe. They had to go back and forth to the US FOB in Baghdad to get warm chow. If not, they had to eat what was on their site. They hired a guy to cook them egg sandwiches or whatever he could out of eggs. By the time you left the site after a year, you would know how to cook eggs a million ways. Well, I guess their cook did the same thing. They made a little area to sit and wait for their delicate sandwiches and encouraged me to get one. It was cold so I did. It kind of reminded me of walking the streets in Korea late at night eating Hotuk, Tokpoki, or their version of a late night burger which consisted of egg too.

Alalima in Baghdad

The division team tried to make it like home as well and if you look closely in the picture to the left, you can see some dying flowers in the window sill. Somebody really missed home. See if you can beat that HGTV! This was one time I was really cold. I love the HGTV and I really missed the Food Network. **Inspiration Verse** Psalm 119:120 "My flesh trembles in fear of you; I stand in awe of your laws."

We had so much trouble along the Tigris with the anti Iraqi forces which was a build up from the summer. Our Iraqi BNs were doing everything to clear and hold that area. It was difficult. At one point we didn't put enough effort to stop them from using the bridge so we took out the bridge. Eric and his team were there on the ground when the planes dropped the bombs but it still rocked us as we sat on our building waiting for the fireworks. It was blown completely in half. Direct hit as we scanned the damage the next day. I recorded it with my camera and we watched it over and over. Good job Air Force.

In Conclusion.

How could you do missions with many that you trusted but knew that there were some in their group that were not trustworthy? There were times the cell phone was used by informants to share small details of non classified information but put together with many other small facts could become sensitive. The US uses Operations Security as a process of identifying essential elements of friendly Information and subsequently analyzing friendly actions. It is used in military operations and other activities (FM 3-13, NOV 2003). The old saying still remains true, "Loose lips sink ships."

CHAPTER TEN

Bread is a Gift

I had nowhere to go. I was trapped with other MiTT members and it was their interpreter that saved me. This group had begun to grow around us as we began to talk football. It wasn't American football because they knew about Soccer, Real Madrid, Ronaldo and Rhonaldhino and the rest of the huge league. At first they didn't know what I was talking about but then I got a piece of warm fresh bread and attempted to kick it as an example of football. Immediately they threw their hands to their faces and said "Allah had given us this bread from Mohammad". I had made the royal mistake of a lifetime.

A guy I work with shared that a general officer once picked a leaf off of a historic tree in a Middle East country and his assistant grabbed him and shoved him in the vehicle before the locals did. He had no idea it meant so much to them. They were going to kill this guy and the crowd was going crazy. This is what I mean by just blowing it.

I Just Wanted To See If They Liked Soccer

I was really embarrassed and completely ruined my chances of speaking with them anymore. They said it is forbidden because I had used my foot, which is one of the dirtiest parts of the body with something sacred. I was truly sorry that I did this one. My interpreter grabbed my arm and pulled me backwards as I grabbed my 9MM and M4 and placed the selector switch from safe to fire. Red is dead!

I thought for sure I was going to die that day. I went back to the HMMWV and waited to leave. I wanted to leave so fast and get the heck out of there. Football was big and I made every effort to build a team. I even got my Iraqi boss to get in on the action when I gave him half of my football. I ran around the compound yelling World Cup 2007 or something and I snatched this photo of him when I gave him his gift. I was a crazy fool.

Soccer Season

The Art Of Making Clay

Most people don't know how much effort goes into making bread anyway. My early years in Goleta showed me that the process may take long, but having the results that you wanted was worth it. My mom Cynthia would pour powdered clay and water into a vat and the machine would mix it all up. When the clay was pushed from the machine, it still needed lots of work before it was ready to throw on the wheel. You had to push it and roll it to get the air out much like bread. After you did that and made your object, taking it to the kiln would be your first test if you got all the air out. If you didn't, the clay would burst or have little bubbles and thin spots on the bowl or vase or whatever you were making. In the bible, it describes vendors who would put wax in the cracks of their pots to fool the merchants. You could only see this by holding the piece in the light. The piece would have to be held in the candle light if in a dark space to reveal its imperfections. One day, we will all be held in the light to see our imperfections. It is a real art form that I will not go into now but the effort of having bread and caring for something that Allah gave the Muslim people is to be cherished. **Inspiration Verse** Psalm 119:122 "Ensure your servant's well-being; let not the arrogant oppress me."

February was also the month I got to learn to drive my first Bradley Vehicle. We took it to the track just outside the US side and went on the hills and straightaway's for my first time. (**TIP 21: When in the presence of friendly forces, be sure to examine their discipline especially putting their finger on the trigger while walking. You want to be sure you don't get shot.**)

We were held up initially because we found some 155MM mortars there and if we ran them over it would have been ugly. After about 30 minutes when EOD arrived they were quickly picked up and we were back in business. That was the fastest I had ever seen them. They were always busy, so I am very grateful. When going up a hill it is important that when you get to the top you gotta gun it or it may stall or flip. I was scared at first but I was in good hands. That was another great day. I had been next to them and seen them operate at night which was something like the terminator. Very scary war machine! Didn't your mommas ever tell you to don't touch? Someone should have told the anti Iraqi forces that because they were no match for that beast. **Inspiration Verse** Psalm 119:123 "My eyes fail, looking for your salvation, looking for your righteous promise."

The Missile Reports Were Accurate

Who was the guy that said there were no weapons of Mass destruction over there? Can someone please send him this photo? There was so much artillery and beat up stuff over there it drove me crazy when I heard those reports. When we traveled around Baghdad, I wanted to make sure I had plenty of memories of what I had seen so I snapped some photos as we drove by a lot of places.

Me On A Rocket

Our Crew

These pics were in Baghdad where the Iraqi leadership for our Iraqi boss was stationed. He looked the part and so we treated him well. I am not sure if it was the peace sign or the dark shades on the General that made this all cool. My Kids like this picture the most.

Hanging With The General

Determination from the Heart

He has clearly the best gym in El Paso, his students are decorated, and he is willing to teach. He spoke of being a jockey as a young man and all the different experiences he had while growing up in Texas. It may be the desire to compete and be the best possible even when life hasn't dealt the best of cards in his hand. He spoke of watching Bruce Lee when he was younger at one of his exhibitions and being motivated to be a practitioner or the martial arts and teach others the way of defense. Despite all the success, life hasn't always been this way. He was forced to give up his heart as a young man because it didn't work well due to an accident and live with the alternative man made one. Early in his life he dealt with pain and let downs. With all the heart trouble and the replacement heart, he still has constant pain. He still moves on and inspires others to be their best. Even when some kids can't afford the lessons, they still let some children come and practice because they know what it means to be dedicated and have discipline at such a young age. With a heart of willingness to move on and teach others to be champions, it is what we should strive to be everyday.

Master Meek is the best Tae Kwon Do instructor in El Paso and he does it by determination to live. We should take a page out of his book and become masters of the art of determination. Thanks for being a great role model both you and Lydia.

In Conclusion.

Information Operations consists of other supporting and related capabilities. A related capability is Civil Military Operations: the activities of a commander that establish, maintain, influence, or exploit relations between military forces, governmental and nongovernmental civilian organizations and authorities, and the civilian populace (JP 3-13, FEB 2006). One of the benefits of being on the staff was integrating the Civil Affairs team which oversaw the rebuilding of many of the city's infrastructure. Watching the sewage lines being fixed, the electricity being turned on, or schools being built was a tremendous victory for their people. These actions that supported the commander developed trust and confidence within the local populace that supported the government and the legitimacy of its actions.

CHAPTER ELEVEN

Marzo

I think our boss was gone in March so we were all very excited. It was because we thought we could get a little break. He was always out trying to make things happen and make a good situation into a better one. When he would come into the TOC, I would really try to do my best for fear that he would say it wasn't good enough. After a mission, if I wasn't there doing a storyboard or writing a report, he would let me know to get started and begin to build better reports. He would have someone go around the area and go find me. Despite having instructions on the storyboards and what to do, he had the best interests in mind. Sometimes that kind of pressure is just the kind that makes people go crazy. So when he left, we all were so excited for the break. Don't take it personally Stan because you were the best we had and thank God we all came home. **Inspiration Verse** Psalm 119:125 "I am your servant; give me discernment that I may understand your statutes."

Taxi Service To The Rescue

That quickly ended when he called us from Baghdad about three weeks later telling us to come and pick him up. The acting 1SG came and told me the news. I said "not on my dead body" because it was a high risk assessment just to drive for one guy who could easily take a helicopter ride in 20 minutes. When I told our smart guy Ross he made a big hoopla but there was never any wind in his sail. Either that or he would just pull over at the shore and catch a cab. He was like that. I couldn't blame him because half of the guys on my team didn't volunteer before their retirement to go to Iraq if you get my drift. So I remember when he came in on the helicopter and he was really mad. Who cares because we didn't want to get killed for one guy but he thought we were his limousine service. Not that day. **Inspiration Verse** Psalm 119:130 "The unfolding of your words gives light; it gives understanding to the simple."

My interpreters knew that before long we would all be saying goodbye to one another. There were several that wanted to show their gratitude to us and planned a cookout. We ate again and grilled some of the food they made for us. We ate and ate until I couldn't eat anymore. They even took pictures of my flag with them so they could feel what it was like to be an American. They really wanted to come back with us and serve in the US to get away from the horror of everyday life. I couldn't blame them for wanting to leave. Everything you see on TV about living in neighborhoods with checkpoints at each corner was true. How could you get by a Sunni neighborhood if you were Shia? Life was rougher for them than I will ever know.

One interpreter brought me clothes for me and my family. I thought the gesture was amazing. They wanted me to remember them and pray for their safety. I thought the best of them when they did this for me. We took a lot of pictures and laughed at the crazy year we just had. We also ate and drank chai together. They really liked it when I gave them candy and stuff. If you can get a Hershey's Kiss into a marshmallow before you cook it, it is almost as good as a Smore with crackers.

I think that when this country experiences the affects of having many of their brightest countrymen leave and go to other countries for refuge, they lose the best of their future. Many that leave are brilliant people who just want to get away from the fighting and killing that goes on all around them. Those that leave can't help but feel the obligation to one day return and make it a better place. It is a terrible thing when you have to leave everything you ever knew, homes, family, friends and even the treasures of your heart in order to start over. I hope many return and change the country for the best.

In Conclusion.

It is extremely important that the leaders of Iraq at every level realize the good that their government is trying to establish. It is true that many leaders that stay in Iraq are in danger and many of those that leave will return to see brighter days. It is difficult in many ways to accomplish the goals of Iraq and they must be engaged at every level. This is why the Public Affairs has an incredible role in telling the truth of what is going on in the unit, to the community and to the public (JP 3-13, Feb 2006). The Iraqi Government and the legitimacy of the gov does hinge on the press in so many ways. Of course, bad articles do hurt them but the truth will always come out.

CHAPTER TWELVE

April

We were getting pretty annoying to the US BDE by this time when we would send up our reports and I had to deal with this at the BDE meetings every day. "Why are you going into another units sector?" asked the leadership. It was funny because our boss had always showed up at the right time. Once out of our sector we had cordoned off the area for a kidnapper and we were the first ones on the scene before the other US units. The US BDE CDR would always have this funny look on his face. When our boss was out in no man's land where anti Iraqi forces were good at hiding mortars used to shoot at our FOB or US troops, our boss was there calling in ATK AVN. He would make the 6 o'clock news at the BUBs (Battle Update Briefs) and then everyone would say "Great Job" Scorpion3. I would shrug my shoulders and laugh like a hyena inside. It was just too comical. **(TIP 22: Spending time with Iraqis and learning the language will build great friendships).**

The Lone Ranger

When our boss said this one particular time to go on the other side of the Tigris River on the east side and look into some potential AIF (Anti Iraqi Forces) that did a lot of kidnappings in our interpreters area, we were on the hunt. We were also looking for additional EFPs like the ones that went through our boss's armored HMMWV. So it was justifiable but still risky. When is it not risky? It was always risky.

Inspiration Verse Psalm 119:133 "Direct my footsteps according to your word; let no sin rule over me."

I was sitting in our TOC one afternoon and I heard we had another Iraqi soldier hit at the front of the gate by the local Market. When he came into the Iraqi hospital after being rushed by their medics, he looked worse. I can't forget the scene I saw there that had unfolded. There were so many male doctors nurses that were bending over this guy doing that and cleaning this on the man. You know it is over when the doc looks at his watch or clock, takes off his sterile gloves and throws them in the trash. Despite getting on the man and doing CPR and IVs to his arms, his time had come. I stood there in the doorway with the curtain open in the little bed where he lie and just stared at the scene. It was weird and surreal being on this side of life and just minutes ago that soldier was with us too. So I looked up at the clock as if copying the doctor as seen many times on ER or late night shows for the time of death and then it hit me. **Inspiration Verse** Psalm 119:135 "Make your face shine upon your servant and teach me your decrees."

Here I was looking at another Iraqi soldier who just gave his life ultimately for his country, for his freedom and everyone else who he served. It was a powerful and profound moment. Well I had read many times and heard or seen the verse from the Bible about John 3:16 and not just from the famous Florida football player or professional wrestler, but it really hit me. It was a somewhat overcast day, getting to the point where it wasn't hot yet in Iraq but still quite pleasant. The words jumped off their page as if speaking from the dead man's life to mine. "For God so loved the world that He gave His only begotten Son, that whosoever should believe in Him would not perish, but have everlasting life" (The NASB).

From that moment I knew that this man had given the ultimate sacrifice for his country and comrades and that the God of the Universe had done the same for me. I know it mattered in Gods eyes that he died in a lonely uncomforted way with none of his family or brothers to hold his hand or stroke his head before breathing his last. What mattered most is if this man would see God when he opened his eyes. It was a scary thought. In Iraq where I lived, there were no Jesus bumper stickers, no Jesus Radio, no Jesus on the corner or Jesus flyers that some guy was passing out standing on a box, or any type of Judeo Christian memorabilia, church, choir singing, Gideon Bible volunteer passing out anything. It was just an incredible void of any type of this activity. If you wanted to live that way, I can tell you that it was very difficult. **Inspiration Verse** Psalm 119:138 "The statutes you have laid down are righteous; they are fully trustworthy."

Alone In My Room

Many nights and afternoons I would just go to my room and close the door and put on a CD to get me through. I listened to an Aaron Shust "Anything Worth Saying" CD that I bought in the PX and nearly wore it out. First of all I couldn't believe that his CD was there in Iraq. There is a song on the CD that I clung to called: "Give it all away" that I listened over and over. It reminded me of the man on that hospital gurney and how he gave everything he had for his country. This song talks about taking all of my plans, dreams, time laying at His feet and submitting to the One that dared to give it all away for me. I listened to it over and over and just wanted to do my best for Him at that moment. If you say I had a religious experience then I am fine with that. But it's hard to feel alive because of the callousness and death. Every day I saw the craziest kinds of things there in Iraq. At some point there is a realization that all of this will pass away and that I am at war internally as well as in the current surroundings. Thanks Aaron for the great memories and moments I had in that hole of a bed room. Maybe it was an upper room experience because I was literally living on the second floor?

Will It Ever End For Them?

There was another time that I realized the pain of what I saw in a man's eyes. We were traveling along the Tigris again and I was the gunner of the M240 and we happened to hear a lot of gunfire. We got word from the Iraqis that some AIF were out causing trouble in a palm grove. We heard there was one casualty. This man sat against the wall crying while I drove by. The other men were bringing the body on a stretcher. The man on the stretcher was his brother just a few feet away. The utter look of pain on his face couldn't be described by my words. I thought of all the good times I had with my brother and still think about if a moment like that ever happened to me. It makes me sad to think of such thoughts so I try not to. **Inspiration Verse** Psalm 119:141 "Though I am lowly and despised, I do not forget your precepts."

This was the month that we were preparing to get the heck out of Dodge. I could feel the tension begin to release and the disappointment of not doing missions drove our boss crazy. He was itching for that feeling again. It was gonna be good when we left and I started working on my changing of the guard SOPs (Standard Operating Procedures) for the next green guy. I wanted to make sure he had no questions and planned out all the dates and times I and the rest of our team would pass the baton to the next MiTT.

In Conclusion.

The integration of Information Operations does not end with the relief in place or transfer of authority. It is at this time that coordination prior to this event should be made with the incoming and new staff. Those lessons learned of the environment will help the staff integrate those lessons into their plans from inception, it will help mitigate unintended circumstances, integrate IO into the base plans and orders, and assist the commander in understanding and visualizing the informational aspects of the operating environment (Core Functions of the G/S7).

CHAPTER THIRTEEN

Cinco De Mayo

I can't believe its May already. Instead of beautiful birds flying overhead and a song in my step, there were no birds but flies and mosquitoes. It still stunk from the lake of sewage at our doorstep and there was only chanting from the loudspeakers overhead with the morning and afternoon prayers. I did learn that it is quite important and meaningful to say to one another "Salam Alekum, Wa alekum Salam" when greeting someone. I wish we had something like that in the states rather than getting the bird flashed at you when experiencing some common road rage. If I said may the light be upon you or God Bless you to someone they would get that look and want to say you're crazy. You know the look, "take your dumb happy self and your dumb comment and go hug a tree or something". Too bad we can't do something like that in the states. In the south where I went to school and lived for about nine years, we would wave when driving by someone or give them the two finger wave on the steering wheel. It never caught on when I did it to the Iraqis or driving around.

Moving On Up

So our acting 1SG had made all the arrangements and we began to check out mentally. We got some rooms on the US FOB just days before they arrived and it was like being a new man. I couldn't believe how hot the water was or not smelling and not missing chow for those

15 days. Life was good again so I thought. I just didn't want to bite the bullet on the way out. "God, please take care of me while I am in the last leg." **Inspiration Verse** Psalm 119:143 "Trouble and distress have come upon me, but your commands are my delight." **(TIP 23: When conversing about your family, be very careful not to ask about their wives or girls. This can be very offensive).**

When I first arrived to my room in the White House, I was sharing a room with Marlon and it wasn't so bad but I wanted my own room. When I got my room several months later I had nothing in it but a mattress and frame. I went and got some tables and chairs and had a coffee table made for me by the unit carpenter. When I gave him nails and tools he did it for free. This little Iraqi man had one of those little toy hammers that was like a tear drop but had nowhere to pull nails and he could build anything with that. It is amazing how resourceful you can be with not having much but this guy was awesome. So my room ended up having a desk and some shelves that he made for me.

When I was leaving, I gave it all to my interpreters who were so thankful. If they wanted to take it to their home or sell it, I didn't care. I just wanted my room clean. When the rest of the Soldiers on the US side did the same thing, they just threw their stuff in the dumpsters. It was like being in college when I saw this the last time. My interpreters eyes bulged out and they wanted to go dumpster diving, trash digging, toilet grabbing. It didn't matter to them but they didn't mind getting the stuff and turning a profit. I would take this Chevy or Cheby truck as my homeboy might say to the dumpsters at night and load up. I felt like Fred Sanford but Iraqi style. No kidding it was a trip. **Inspiration Verse** Psalm 119:146 "I call out to you; save me and I will keep your statutes."

Look, Nothing For You

The rest of the replacements went to their rooms and saw all the stuff and were like "cool beans". Some of our guys were selling stuff as packages like lamps, radios, carpets, etc so they could make a buck. I heard the excitement from the new guys as they went through the rooms. When my replacement came to my room and saw it was clean as silk, his jaw dropped and he was like Santa never brought him any presents. He was so broken and bent out of shape that he made one comment to me and that was it. He let it out and then for the next 10 days just held his tongue. I didn't feel bad because my terps gave all they had for us so why couldn't I do the same. No sweat but I should have left my replacement more. If you are reading this, oops, I goofed, sorry. **(TIP 24: Treating the Leader with much respect will be very productive. Honoring them is a way of life).**

I was glad that through it all I had a relative I could come and hang out for a while. Jessie Tafoya was the son of my uncle so I went to make sure he was doing fine. He gave me lots of coffee from Starbucks and made sure I wasn't short on medical supplies. We ate every now and then and got to know one another better.

Before we left I knew that the times would be difficult for the next team. When we took them out for their battlefield circulation, they saw firsthand what it would be like when people got hurt. One guy that was injured ran right by me and my replacement. The blood was all over him and then I knew they thought it would be a wild ride for them too. I am glad they all made it out alive. The only bad thing for me was that I hurt my back again when we got to Baghdad. I didn't realize that I was carrying over 200 pounds of ammo, gear, clothing and junk and it threw me for a loop. I spent my first night in Kuwait waiting to get some pain killers because I couldn't stand up straight. My team had to help me again. Now, all my team could watch me get sent home. I had no problem with that.

Learning about the other culture was a very eye opening experience for me and one I will never forget. We learn from our experiences and hope for the best for those that we impacted. Thank God I made it back, thank God I made it.

The realization that their country will be just that, their country! Who can really change things in their new army except them? We can provide a way of doing things but it may not be their way. We can show them how we did it but it might not be their way, even after years of fighting. The schools, the hospitals, the roads, the legal system, the economy are all driven by Iraqis and their vision of tomorrow. We can only share how we did it in the US but ultimately it is their decision to have their democracy the way they like it. Either in a fast food venue or a dinner by the fire. Whatever the event, it is their time to be responsible for their actions, their lifestyle, their country, and their future.

IN CLOSING

The Story Continues

Don't be a roasted marshmallow. This is the part that every Soldier must deal with when returning back to the states. I got several tickets that first month by the local police and got no slack from the officers that ticketed me. I told them where I just came from and they said I didn't look the dangerous type. I was shocked inside but knew they saw nothing compared to what I just came from.

When the time slows down and it is so quiet in your room that your ears are ringing like a constant bell, be sure to let your frustration and anger out properly. Don't be the tough guy and hold it in. There is nothing wrong with seeing a shrink. The important thing is getting your thoughts and heart right. If you know someone that is struggling, don't be afraid to be an ear to lean on. This may save his life. PTSD comes in many different ways after deployment. You got to remember that you are human and we all break down and need a good charge of our batteries. Speaking to a Chaplain or someone who can listen and help you is your best reward. Don't forget to reward yourself and invest in yourself. You are the most important thing on earth! When you get to Afghanistan or go to Iraq, don't forget to Roast Marshmallows for me!

BIBLIOGRAPHY

Joint Pub 3-13, Information Operations, Feb 2006.

FM 3-0, Operations, Feb 2008.

FM 3-13, Information Operations: Doctrine, Tactics, Techniques, and Procedures, 2003.

FM 3-05.30, Psychological Operations, April 2005.

Overview of Information Operations and Army

Information Tasks, Core Functions of the G/S7, Slide Show, US Army IO Proponent, Leader Development, Education, and Training Division, FA30 Qualification Course, Fort Leavenworth, Kansas

Psychological Operations, Slide Show, US Army IO Proponent, Leader Development, Education, and Training Division, FA30 Qualification Course, Fort Leavenworth, Kansas.

Charles Taylor Information, pulled from the internet site at (http://en.wikipedia.org/wiki/Charlie_Taylor).

Creating An MOE, Slide Show, US Army IO Proponent, Leader Development, Education, and Training Division, FA30 Qualification Course, Fort Leavenworth, Kansas.

New American Standard Bible.

Ten Lessons in Leadership from a Janitor "website on the internet.